MUSIC
SAVED
my LIFE

One Printers Way
Altona, MB R0G 0B0
Canada

www.friesenpress.com

Copyright © 2022 by Grant H. Reynolds
First Edition — 2022

All rights reserved.

No part of this publication may be reproduced in any form, or by any means, electronic or mechanical, including photocopying, recording, or any information browsing, storage, or retrieval system, without permission in writing from FriesenPress.

ISBN
978-1-03-913989-3 (Hardcover)
978-1-03-913988-6 (Paperback)
978-1-03-913990-9 (eBook)

1. BIOGRAPHY & AUTOBIOGRAPHY, COMPOSERS & MUSICIANS

Distributed to the trade by The Ingram Book Company

FOR STEVE AND JULIE

MUSIC SAVED MY LIFE

How I Survived My Parents, A Difficult
Marriage, Crazy Religion, and Being Gay

GRANT H. REYNOLDS

I remember finally getting to be pianist at the Arcadian Court, an elegant dining room with beautiful chandeliers and a clientele that came there to dine and hear me play. One day a man came up to the piano and said, "We think you're wonderful!" His face was familiar, but it took me a few moments to realize it was Ken Thomson, the richest man in Canada and the son of the man for whom Roy Thomson Hall was named. I received so much praise from people like him who came to hear me play, and I got so much joy from being immersed in music. I loved my life!

Unfortunately, it wasn't always that way…

TABLE OF CONTENTS

CHAPTER 1

Born Into a Cold Climate

Several years ago, I decided to organize all my photos. I bought a huge album with space for dates, events, locations, and names beside the photos. It was a big task because I had drawers full of photos, but I set my timer to work on it for just ten minutes every day as part of my morning routine. Sometimes I got so involved that I went at it for much longer. In a year or two, my album was complete.

The first photograph in the album is of me at a few months old, beaming as I take my first steps supported by my "Aunt" Audrey. She's looking down at me with such delight and excitement that I'm convinced she's just as thrilled at my fabulous new skills as I am!

I seldom saw delight on my own mother's face. In my other baby photos, if she is present, we are never touching. She has a slight smile but is very reserved and appears slightly uncomfortable.

Mother never shared emotion with me, or told me she loved me, or praised me, or touched me affectionately. Although she was usually gentle, seldom got angry, and did everything she possibly could for me, something was missing—and I felt that lack every day. A few years ago, I read that if a mother doesn't respond to the emotions of her child, the child may stop expressing or even feeling those emotions.

During my first few years I gradually became more and more withdrawn. Of course, I couldn't analyze what was wrong at the time. In most of my twenty-five years of psychotherapy, I focused on my father as the reason why no matter what I achieved, I could never feel fulfilled and happy. Now I realize that my mother also contributed significantly to my feeling emotionally dead and unable to connect with people.

When I was young, Mother told me she disapproved of "sentimentality." Years later, when her daughter-in-law's father died, she complained about her crying so much over his death. My brother said that when he told Mother that Princess Diana had died, all she said was, "Well, she was a problem for the royal family."

Once, I asked Mother why she wasn't more expressive. She was uncomfortable but reluctantly admitted that she'd always had trouble expressing emotion. She told me that when she was young, she went to a birthday party with some other little girls. The father of the birthday girl took them all to a movie. Afterwards, he asked Mother's parents if something was wrong because all the other little girls had laughed and emoted, but Mother just sat impassively throughout the entire show.

Mother's religion undoubtedly increased her cerebral approach to life. A devout Christian Scientist, she had to avoid getting emotional so that her mind would always be clear to deny what the senses were telling her. She believed that focus on the physical made one less "spiritual" and therefore less able to connect to God and have access to healing.

My parents grew up in Winnipeg and married there in 1942. Dad didn't fight in the war. Instead, as a chemical engineer, he came to Nobel, Ontario to make munitions. I was born in 1944. After the war, on my first birthday, November 15, 1945, Mother and I were on the train to join Dad, who, unable to get a job in Winnipeg, had found a position in Toronto with the Ontario Department of Health.

The years immediately after the war were tough for most people. My parents bought an old farmhouse on Bridgeland Avenue in a run-down area of North York. A big industrial garage sat on the property, which they rented out to a couple who had a son a little older than me. On the property there was also an abandoned chicken coop, which my Uncle Van, an architectural student, remodelled to live in with his wife, my Aunt Nancy. All three couples were in the process of building nicer homes in better areas of North York.

To augment their income, my parents kept chickens and sold eggs. I can remember petting the cute little chicks when they arrived and then crying out when I went to pet the full-size chickens and got my fingers pecked. I also remember seeing Dad holding a chicken's neck down on a stump with one arm and awkwardly wielding an axe with the other to cut its head off. It made me sad, but I was also fascinated to see a headless chicken run around in circles.

When I was four, I started kindergarten, walking to the bus with a neighbour, Jimmy, who was my age. It seemed like quite a long walk along Bridgeland Avenue to Dufferin, where we got the TTC bus to C.B. Parsons School. One day on the way to the bus, we saw flowers in a front garden and picked some for our teacher. Another time we stopped to eat some cake someone had put out in their garbage at the end of their driveway.

We moved to the new house when I was six, and I had another long walk to my new school. My Grade 1 teacher was Miss Reese. She had grey hair and dark circles around her eyes and never smiled. If one student misbehaved, we *all* had to sit on our hands. When she got upset, she yelled at us, went into the coat closet, shut the door, and in a couple of minutes emerged calmer. Once, when my classmate Johnny was making his desk squeak by rocking back and forth, she came over to him and screamed, "If you like noise so much, let's see how much noise you can make!" Then she grabbed both sides of the desk and violently shook it up and down until Johnny's nose hit the desk and started bleeding. When Miss Reese saw the blood she stopped shaking the desk, and looking worried, got some tissue for him. Her violence was terrifying to me.

One of the first experiences I remember in the new house was having a temper tantrum at the dinner table. I don't remember what it was about, but I was sent to my room. While there, I climbed from my top bunk bed to the closet shelf, where there was a clock that my grandmother had given me. Sobbing, I smashed its glass face. No one came to talk to me, and nothing was ever said about the incident. It was if it had never happened. I was left with a residue of guilt and shame. That night I retreated into myself even more and resolved to hold everything inside and never show any emotions again.

Around this time, I experienced something that will forever be engraved in my mind. I was in our back yard playing "doctor" with several of the neighbourhood kids. Suddenly Mother, who had never been anything but gentle with me, appeared and raced toward me, grabbing my arm and roughly dragging me into the bathroom, where she washed out my mouth with soap. She then pulled me into my room and shut the door. Not a word was said, but I got the message that I had done something unforgivably evil.

A school was built close to my new house in time for me to start Grade 2 there. I was very shy and didn't know how to make friends. The other boys loved recess because they could play games, but I never joined them. I just stood by myself, feeling more and more uncomfortable, and waited until recess was finally over. This went on for my entire elementary school education.

Every Sunday, Mother took us to the Christian Science Sunday school. I gradually became indoctrinated and came to believe that sickness was just an illusion and could be healed by clearly seeing that we are a reflection of God and therefore cannot be sick. To please Mother, I chose not to get vaccinated and sat by myself in the classroom while all the other pupils filed out to get their vaccinations.

When my Grade 2 teacher taught us about religions, we each had to state our religion. I knew that my religion wasn't acceptable, so, unlike the other kids, I went up to my teacher and whispered, "Christian Science" in her ear. One day I got very sick at school and my teacher tried to give me an aspirin. I strenuously refused it because I had been taught in Sunday school that pills only made you sicker and led you away from God.

Although Mother was usually kind, a few times, without any warning she threw out devastating criticisms that wounded me to the core. One evening when I was in Grade 8, she came home from a parents' night at my school and said with a terribly troubled look, "The shop teacher asked me if you were manually deficient!" She then left the room. I was in shock. Suddenly I felt like a total failure and that all the good marks I got in my other subjects meant nothing. And for me they did mean nothing. Shop was my only "masculine" subject, and to fail at it was to fail as a boy.

On another occasion, Mother came into the house and blurted out, "Mr. Ross says you swing a baseball bat like a girl." I didn't know what to say. I was so hurt. Again I felt I'd failed as a boy. I had no masculinity and no dignity. I was overcome with shame.

I never saw Mother be unkind to anyone else, and recently I've wondered why she was so cruel to me on those occasions. The only thing I can think of is that secretly she despised me because I didn't measure up to the standards she had for a boy. Being so repressed, she buried her feelings deep and every once in a while they suddenly erupted.

When I was about twelve, a woman who had heard me play the piano invited Mother and me to a Toronto Symphony concert. After it ended and we had said goodbye to her, all Mother said to me was, "Did you have to keep your mouth open the whole time?" I didn't realize how much this comment affected me until years later when a psychologist tried to get me to stop clamping my jaws together.

Only my failures were pointed out, never my successes. And no suggestions for how to be better were ever given. My emotions simmered, but nothing came to the surface. It was all repressed, and there was no resolution of any problems. Feelings were buried deeper and deeper.

CHAPTER 2

Distant Dad

Dad was born in 1915. Entering the job market during the Great Depression and being unable to find a job shaped him. He fixed everything himself and bought only cheap things that often didn't work. He bought a gas lawn mower that would run a short time then stop, and then you'd have to vigorously yank the throttle rope to start it again. I often persisted with this lawn mower because I always wanted to please him. I can't recall him ever thanking me or even acknowledging the lawn cutting. Once, when I was at another boy's house, I heard his mother say to him, "Your father called and said to thank you for cutting the lawn. He said you did a great job." I felt a tinge of sadness because I didn't have a father like that.

After my mother died in 2002, my brothers gave me all her photos and asked me to make an album of her life. Among the photos, I was surprised to discover one of me at about age two sitting on my father's shoulders. This surprised me because I don't remember him ever having physical contact with me. Also in the photograph are his parents on a rare visit from Winnipeg, and I realize he may have been playing father to impress them.

My father and I had no connection whatsoever. He never spoke to me, not even a "Hi." It troubled me deeply. Once, when I was alone with Mother, I couldn't contain myself and blurted out, "Dad doesn't love me."

"Yes, he does," she replied.

"No, he doesn't!" I yelled.

When she realized how upset I was, a troubled look came over her face and she reluctantly said, "Well, he is ... selfish." That gave me some comfort because Mother seldom criticized people, and *never* Dad. However, what I really needed was for her to simply put her arm around me and say, "I love you," which unfortunately she was incapable of doing.

Mother was right. Dad was selfish—and to an extent I've never seen in any other person. He never showed compassion or pity, except for himself. When he complained about having to make money to support us, he looked as if he was going to cry. I felt I was just a burden, "another mouth to feed."

Apart from the time Mother admitted Dad was selfish, I never saw her criticize, challenge, or make fun of him. She once told us that she was so impressed with him early in their relationship because the car broke down and he dealt with the problem without showing any anger. I couldn't believe she would say that without a trace of irony because Dad was the angriest person I'd ever encountered. He often had a scowl on his face and threw horrible temper tantrums.

One terrifying temper tantrum occurred before Christmas. Dad always bought a real tree and decorated it himself. One year, he ended up with a decidedly lopsided tree and nailed it to the stand, but it fell over. He kept trying different ways to balance the tree, but after several failures, he suddenly went ballistic. Screaming curses, snarling, and waving his hammer wildly through the air, he grabbed four spikes and bashed one through each end of the wooden stand and right into the hardwood floor. He was so furious and out of control, I was afraid he would bash me with the hammer accidentally. Afterwards there was dead silence. None of us dared to move or speak. We all pretended it had never happened.

Another major tantrum I recall derived from an electrical problem. After repeatedly being unable to get an appliance to work, screaming and cursing, he took a glass fuse in his hand, raised his arm high, and with all his might hurled it onto the ceramic tile in front of the fireplace. The glass broke in many tiny pieces. Mother tried to show no expression, but I still remember the troubled look on her face as she patiently swept the bits of glass into the dustpan. Again, nothing was ever said about this at the time or later.

Dad seemed to dislike people, and I was ashamed of his obvious hostility. I remember a heavy woman crossing the street in front of our car and him muttering, "Move it, fatty, or I'll put a dent in you!"

I was invited to go to a cottage for a week with my schoolmate, Jimmy, and his family. I had so much fun! My parents never acted silly, but after we all got into our beds and the lights were turned out, Jimmy's parents would tell funny stories, and at the punch lines I would laugh myself silly and relax into sleep as I never did at home.

Every day, Jimmy and I went to the tuck shop to have an ice-cream cone, and the friendly woman who served us would chat with us. She was very dramatic, which fascinated me. I'll never forget the time she asked Jimmy if his family had bought a ticket for the camp raffle. Jimmy replied, "Oh, no! Gambling is against our religion." In her low, smoky voice the woman informed him,

"Honey, *life's* a gamble."

Jimmy's family was staying at the cottage for two weeks, so at the end of my week, my parents came to pick me up and take me home. Before we left, Dad needed cigarettes, so he went to the tuck shop with Jimmy and me, who were going to get our last ice cream cone together. The woman who worked in the tuck shop tried to make conversation with Dad, and when she found out he was my father, she told him how polite I was and commented on how proud of me he must be. Dad didn't say a word, and when I looked over, I saw an angry scowl on his face. The friendlier she got, the angrier he looked. I felt terrible. I wondered what was wrong. Did her friendly talk mask evil intentions I could not yet perceive? I went home very troubled—a sad ending to my enjoyable week.

Recently I read about a form of anxiety that causes a person to need detachment from all emotions and emotional ties with others. This perfectly describes my father.

Even though Dad tended not to talk to *me*, at dinner he would hold forth in front of us all. Like any child, I wanted to learn about life, so I absorbed what Dad said, but later when I would express a similar viewpoint, he would say the opposite of his previous position. When I'd get frustrated and upset, he'd get a crooked smile on his face and say, "I was just being devil's advocate." After a few episodes like this, I stopped attempting to have a sincere conversation with him.

Because Dad never showed any tenderness, I came to see tenderness as weak and shameful. I once saw the older boy across the street fall off his bike and start crying. When his father came over and picked him up, I was disgusted at the boy's weakness for crying (which I never did, no matter what the pain) and the father's tenderness (which I had come to see as not masculine).

When the man next door had an inground pool installed, he invited the neighbourhood boys over to swim. None of us wanted to go in because the water was freezing, so he threw a silver dollar into the pool. Even though there were older boys, only I was brave enough to dive into the ice-cold water and stay down long enough to pick it up. I should have kept it, but I threw it back, thinking the other boys would like me more for it.

My Grade 7 teacher, Mr. Barber, said something to me that I've never forgotten: "Grant, you don't need to apologize for living." He said it with a compassionate look and tone of voice. I didn't understand then what the expression meant, but I felt his concern for me. He obviously noticed I was very troubled.

Despite my attempts to feel nothing when I was young, the most commonplace tenderness can overwhelm me now, especially between fathers and sons. Recently I was walking along the sidewalk when, ahead of me, I saw a father touch his young son on the head affectionately. I was so moved I had to fight not to cry. As I watched the film *Monster's Ball* and saw the father tell his son that he hated him, and then the son replied, "Well, I always loved *you*," and killed himself, I was absolutely overcome with emotion.

Connections

I did have some warm relationships when I was young. The first was with Granny. My maternal grandmother was a Christian Science practitioner. She lived in Winnipeg but visited us a few times, and later she came to live in Toronto for a while. She was warm and outgoing—very different from my mother. I couldn't figure out how a mother and daughter could be so different, but I did notice that people like Granny, who didn't start out as Christian Scientists but came to the religion later in life, tended to be much warmer than those brought up in the faith. (Another example was "Aunt" Audrey, who also came into the religion later in life.)

I loved Granny. She radiated love. People were drawn to her and followed her around. When she came to Toronto, she lived with my aunt and uncle, a block away from us, and was a crossing guard for a while. All the kids loved her. I actually felt slightly jealous. After all, she was *my* grandmother, not theirs. She had been a classical singer, involved in the arts scene in Winnipeg. I can still recall her dramatic reading of bedtime stories and poems. Over and over, I'd ask her to read the poem, "The Wee,

Wee Mannie and the Big, Big Coo," which she did with a great deal of expression and a hilarious Scottish accent!

Unlike my parents, she shared her feelings and life experience with me. She told me that her parents had died when she was young, and she'd gone to live with her grandmother, who overheard her say in her grief, "I wish I were dead!" Her grandmother, horrified, said, "Don't let me ever hear you talk like that again!" I loved her drama and emotion. I can still hear her voice after all these years. She made me feel loved and connected— wonderful feelings I never got from my parents.

The other warm relationship I had was with Audrey and her husband, Joe. Whenever they visited, I felt happy. They were like family, even though Audrey was just a distant relative. (When she was a young woman and went to Winnipeg to study, she stayed with Granny and her daughters, and she and Mother became very close.) Unfortunately, Audrey and Joe lived in Montreal, so they didn't visit very often. Once they came to Toronto and announced that they were going to take their son and my brother and me to the Canadian National Exhibition. We had a great time going on the various rides. My parents never took us anywhere, claiming that Toronto was too crowded and expensive—unlike Winnipeg, where they had grown up and could canoe and skate without crowds and for free.

When my mother was in the hospital giving birth to my youngest brother, Audrey came to look after us. Once she had us all join hands and skip to the store to buy treats. It didn't seem very masculine to me, but it was actually fun. (I don't recall either of my parents ever holding each other's hands, or holding my hand, or going on a walk with us, never mind skipping!)

Joe, not my dad, taught me to ride a bicycle. I'll never forget him running alongside, supporting my two-wheeler as I pedalled furiously until magically I was riding along all by myself, at last able to balance the bike and keep from falling off. Joe was a heavy smoker, and I was aware of his struggle to keep running fast, but I never saw anger or irritation on his face. I always felt a bond with him. He seemed to like me—a feeling I never got from my own dad.

CHAPTER 4

Piano Lessons

I remember coming back to school after lunch one day when I was in Grade 2. I entered the gym with a couple of other boys, and a girl was playing the piano. I froze. The boys asked what was wrong, but I was so paralyzed by the beauty of the music, I couldn't even answer. A short time later, I heard a man playing a ragtime piece. Again, I stopped in my tracks. It was thrilling, catchy, and syncopated, just like the rock and roll I would later play by ear and love.

When I was seven, I started taking piano lessons. When Granny heard, she said, "Wonderful! You'll be the most popular boy at parties!" I knew it wasn't true, but she believed it, and her enthusiasm made me feel great.

Right away I loved playing the piano because, even with the simple pieces I started with, I was able to express my feelings through the music. At my first recital my teacher gave me the prize for the student who had progressed the most. Unfortunately, she didn't believe in conservatory exams or playing in competitions. According to her, playing piano was just for pleasure, and she gave me popular music rather than music that would develop my piano technique. It wasn't until high school that I got a new teacher who had me taking exams, entering competitions, and really progressing. However, I could never make up for those missing years.

Both Mom and Dad had taken piano lessons as children, and after I began my lessons, Dad started taking lessons in popular music. I remember him playing a song called "Margie," the melody in the right hand and a pattern of stride playing in the left. He would get faster and faster until he started hitting wrong chords. Then he'd get angrier and angrier until he was furious and would quit in disgust. He soon stopped taking lessons entirely.

Mother never once touched the piano, although I saw some music that she had studied as a child, and it was quite advanced. When I asked her why she hadn't continued, she just said, "I guess I wasn't very good." When she was young, she was an excellent dancer, featured at Granny's gatherings of the Winnipeg arts community. A famous poet even wrote a verse about her dancing, but I never saw her dance. I suspect both dancing and playing the piano would have embarrassed her because they involved feelings.

A boy named Phil moved in next door and we became friends. I thought he'd go to my school, but he went to a Catholic school. Once, I was sitting with him and his father when his older brother, Lewis, came into the room. Phil's father asked Lewis to recite his catechism. When he didn't know it, his dad slapped his face hard. I was totally shocked because even though Dad was violent with objects, he seldom hit *us*.

We had no TV, but Phil did, and every Saturday morning I would go next door to watch *The Lone Ranger*, *Roy Rogers*, and *Ramar of the Jungle*, all of which I loved. I had asked Dad if we could get a TV, but I got the impression that my request only made him more resistant to the idea.

One Saturday morning when I knocked on Phil's door, his older sister, who was very controlling, opened the door and told me she didn't want me coming to watch their TV anymore. I just exploded, yelling, "I hate you and all your Catholic things!" Her response was to hiss and say, "You'll go to Hell for that!" Her anger upset me, but I wasn't afraid of her threat. One of the good things about Christian Science was that there was no Hell.

I was aware that it was mostly girls who played piano. One day, when I was with Phil and a friend of his, Frank, they asked me to play piano. While I was playing, I heard Frank snicker and realized I was swaying to the music. Later that day, in his yard, Frank threw a hatchet at me. The blade went through my shoe and made a small cut in my heel. The look of satisfaction on his face over his skill at hitting a moving target was far more shocking to me than the injury. I realized that my playing the piano was part of the reason he saw me as a weak sissy, and I would have to be careful in the future.

CHAPTER 5

Non-Demonstrative Parenting

Dad seemed indifferent to me and seldom interacted with me. He never ever called me by my name. I believe that would have been too intimate for him. When I was twelve years old, my voice started changing and would crack every once in a while. One day out of the blue, he called out, *"Hey, Grunt!"* He had a crooked smile on his face, and he repeated it a couple of times. If he'd ever spoken my real name, calling me "Grunt" might not have hurt as much, but I'd been waiting my whole life for him to call me by my name like everybody else did. By that time I was good at not showing any emotion, so I just stared at him and said nothing, wondering what was motivating him. He seemed to get uncomfortable and turned away.

Besides my cracking voice, puberty was upsetting for me in another way. The other boys talked about "jerking off," but when I tried it, even though I had no trouble getting and keeping erections, I couldn't bring myself to orgasm. However, I did have "wet dreams." They would cause me to wake up, remembering the ecstasy and longing to experience orgasm consciously. I was horny much of the time but unable to get a release, and I was terrified someone would find out about my "deficiency."

Around this time, I did something very wrong. Phil and I were playing in the ravine when we encountered a girl who went to my school. She started saying abusive things and daring us to do something about it. I warned her to stop, and when she didn't, Phil and I tied her loosely around the wrists. She didn't seem upset, and we left her there, still taunting us. A couple of hours later, I heard a loud knock on the front door, and then my father and another man talking. I stayed in my bedroom and couldn't make out what they were saying, but I knew it was the girl's father because I could hear the anger in his voice. Dad never spoke to me about it. Once again, there was no resolution of the problem and no learning from it … just shame.

The summer before I started high school, we drove to Winnipeg to visit Aunt Margaret, Mother's older sister, and her husband, my Uncle Bob. I loved staying there because Uncle Bob had a grand piano in a beautiful music room he'd added to the back of his house. He played piano, and he liked my playing, which made me feel great.

One day Uncle Bob and his son Bill and Dad, my brothers, and I headed off to go for a swim. I already had an ear infection and it was getting worse. After our swim, I changed back into my clothes and, delirious, lay down on the grass outside the change room and fell asleep in the sun. I don't know how long I was asleep, but I woke up when I heard voices and then felt a hand on my forehead. It was Uncle Bob checking to see if I had a fever. It felt strange because my parents never touched me, but it also felt good because Uncle Bob clearly cared about me. I was aware of the whole group gathered around me, but Dad was standing at a distance.

When we returned to Toronto in August, a Grade 8 classmate, Josh, approached me and asked what school I was going to in September.

When he found out we were both going to Downsview Collegiate, he suggested meeting and going to our new high school together. I was very nervous about high school, so it would be nice to go with a friend.

When I mentioned to Dad that I wanted to get good marks in high school to please Mother and him, he got a furious look on his face and shouted, "No, you do it for *you*, not for us!" Then Mother rushed into the room and defensively exclaimed, "We care. It's just that *we're not demonstrative*!" They looked at each other with an intensity in their eyes I had never seen before. I felt I had challenged a cherished belief that bonded them together, that they had made a pact, that their lack of demonstrativeness was a *choice*!

They had decided not to "demonstrate" feelings, and they'd succeeded. I never felt loved.

CHAPTER 6

My Horrible Secret

My high school years got off to a very bad start. The day after Labour Day, I walked to Josh's house, and together we headed to Downsview Collegiate for our first day of high school. The school seemed so unfriendly! The teachers called the girls by their first names but the boys by their last names, which they barked out like drill sergeants. Every forty minutes we had to change classrooms. I felt we'd just start to get into a subject and then the bell would ring and we'd have to race to the next classroom. Students carried briefcases, and if you didn't move fast enough, you got one jammed in your rear.

My home form consisted only of boys, many of them repeating Grade 9 and angry about failing. In Phys Ed we had to play floor hockey. I'd never played *any* kind of hockey, and I remember trying to figure out how to stick-handle the cloth "puck" when suddenly one of the big repeaters bodychecked me hard into the wall—so painful! Once, when I was in the washroom in front of a mirror, combing my greased hair to make it look like Elvis Presley's, another repeater in my home form came in and gratuitously yelled, "Reynolds, you're going to fail!"

We had to choose two out of three possible options: music, art, or shop. I chose music, of course, and shop, since I couldn't draw. I recall a welding class when, terrified of injuring my hands and no longer being able to play the piano, I was nervously holding a hot blow torch. My shop teacher, noticing the river of perspiration running into my safety glasses and down my face, yelled, "Reynolds, you've got water on the brain!" Fortunately, after Grade 9 I didn't have to take shop again.

In Grade 9 I took French for the first time. The night before the first test I was outraged that I had to learn to spell a long list of words, but I calmed down eventually and accepted that I had no choice. I studied hard and got a perfect mark. In those days if you didn't pass French, you didn't get a diploma. I soon learned that I could study hard and get top marks in every French test.

In music class I played the clarinet. I had wanted to learn the sax to play rock and roll, but the teacher said I had to master the clarinet first. I didn't like marches and the other music we had to play in the school band, and in five years of high school music, I never did get to play the sax.

However, all my problems paled before the horrible secret I carried: *I was attracted to boys!* I could never relax and be spontaneous. In the pool change room, it was all I could do to not stare at the naked boys. I still have a vivid image in my mind of a very attractive boy standing on a table and drying himself, his crotch within inches of my face. I had a herculean struggle not to get an erection. Meanwhile, all the other boys were relaxed, enjoying standing around talking and laughing as I, a nervous wreck, tried to hide my feelings. My attraction to boys, coupled with my inability to masturbate, made me wonder sometimes if I was being tested to see how much I could take before I cracked. A few years later when I read Margaret Laurence's *A Jest of God*, I thought that the title was a perfect description of me.

I started studying Christian Science more because I thought it might heal me of my unmentionable problems. I tried to read the lesson every day (which took about forty minutes), and I frequently asserted that, as a reflection of God, I couldn't possibly be deficient in any way, nor could I have impure thoughts. The isolation from others and the constant denial of reality were very bad for my mental health. I developed a rash on my right hand that was so itchy I couldn't resist scratching it till it bled.

Christmas held no magic for me. I never felt warmth or excitement or got gifts that I particularly liked. The Christmas after I started high school seemed to follow the usual pattern until I opened a big package and was thrilled to see a clarinet! I thanked my parents vociferously, but they both looked uncomfortable and then Mother said, "Look at the tag." It was from Uncle Bob in Winnipeg. I was mortified!

Because I did well in Grade 9, I was able to get into an enriched program in Grade 10. What an improvement! My new home form was radically different—a roughly equal number of boys and girls, bright, studious, and friendly. I stayed in the enriched program with many of the same students until the end of high school.

Phil and his family moved to a better area, and Anna, a girl in my high school class, moved into his house. We became friends. When she found out what religion I belonged to, she told me of a relative who had contracted a serious illness and, rather than get medical help, sought healing through Christian Science and died. I also heard of a little girl in Winnipeg who was thrown off a horse. Her parents were Christian Scientists and hired a practitioner rather than get medical help, and their little girl died. I couldn't help having doubts about Christian Science when I heard things like that.

CHAPTER 7

My New Life in Music!

Just after I started high school, my piano teacher said I was getting too advanced for her to continue teaching me. I had never taken any exams in piano, but I wanted to get my Grade 8 piano to use as a subject toward my high school diploma, so I started taking lessons with a Royal Conservatory of Music teacher. He was nice but not terribly interested in me or my music. However, he prepared me well and I passed my Grade 8 piano exam.

I started playing popular music, sometimes from sheet music but often by ear. I listened to hit songs like Jerry Lee Lewis's "Great Balls of Fire" and then played the solo part. The other kids in the music class loved hearing me play their favourite pop music before the teacher arrived in class. This helped me to gain a little self-esteem. One day in science class, I got a big laugh from the other students when I played an imaginary version of "Great Balls of Fire" on my desk. The teacher didn't laugh, though. He made me sit under a desk at the front of the classroom for the rest of the period.

I had only one year with the RCM teacher. He said he was returning to New Brunswick and recommended a teacher named John Leberg, who he said was "not an RCM teacher, but very good."

John was in his twenties, had a goatee, and wore sunglasses inside. I thought he was cool! He was so enthusiastic, not just about music, but also about *my* music. I'd just finished my Grade 8 RCM exam, but almost immediately he started preparing me for the Grade 10 exam. He entered me in my first Kiwanis Festival competition: a Beethoven Sonata class. It took place in a church near where Dorothy, a distant relative, lived, so Mother invited her to come along. It was a big class, and I won first place! Dorothy was thrilled, and reminding me of Audrey, flashed the most beautiful smile when I won. Brimming with excitement, she said, "Let's go back to my place and celebrate!" Mother just looked impassive, as usual.

Dad never said a word about my music. Years later, after I'd given my parents an audiotape of my playing, my sister-in-law surprised me by saying, "Your dad sure loves your music!" I wondered why he never told *me* that.

Around this time, I started teaching piano, mostly to beginners. Decades later, a man whom I'd taught when he was a boy came to hear me play at Gatsby's Restaurant and told me he remembered me as a teacher "with a fire in my belly."

Two experiences greatly increased my self-esteem. In Grade 10, I arranged a popular hit, "Exodus," for two pianos, and another pianist and I played it at our school's Music Night. *Exodus* was a current film about the formation of the state of Israel, and we performed the piece with a menorah with lit candles on one of the pianos. The school had a large number of Jewish students, and our performance brought the house down. Sometime afterwards, I was on a bus and I overheard one girl whisper to another, "I think that's the boy who played 'Exodus!'"

The other experience was being asked by three older boys who'd heard me play at music night if I'd join their rock band. I played with them at school dances for a couple of years and got a lot of admiration. However, eventually I got tired of trying to make my piano heard above their loud guitars and drums, so I quit.

When I was in Grade 12, John moved to an apartment at the back of what is now the Keg Mansion. He had two pianos, so we could play concertos. I would play the piano part on one, and he would play the orchestra part on the other. A few times I competed in concerto classes, always with John playing the orchestra part.

My lessons took place on Saturdays and sometimes lasted way beyond the hour I was paying for. John would support me in any repertoire I wanted to play. A man who lived across the street generously gave me a recording titled *Horowitz Plays Chopin*. I loved it, especially the *Ballade in G Minor*. Even though it was very difficult, I asked John if I could play it, and he, as always, was enthusiastic.

Through John I became immersed in music. Having him as my teacher helped me so much. He made me feel valued, praised my playing, and showed me affection—all things I'd hungered for and never received from my parents. He made me believe I had a future in music and got me to think about what I wanted to study in university. Because of him, I was motivated to work hard on geometry, physics, and chemistry—three subjects I had so much trouble with but had to pass in order to get a high school diploma and get into university to study music. There was light at the end of the tunnel.

John was part of Toronto's classical music scene. One morning I got to meet Pierette Lepage and William Aide, two well-known pianists, who dropped in while I was having my lesson. Not long after that, I heard Pierette play Chopin's *Ballade in F Major* on CBC radio and couldn't believe how beautiful and intense the piece, and her playing of it, were.

John took some of his students to Massey Hall to hear William Aide rehearse the Mozart piano concerto he was going to play for his debut performance with the Toronto Symphony Orchestra. Glenn Gould came by and played the piano when the orchestra took a break. I got the world-famous pianist's autograph!

A few years later, John left piano teaching to become director of operations for the Canadian Opera Company under the great Lofti Mansouri, who is famous for inventing surtitles (the English text shown above the stage) so that we can understand an opera sung in a foreign language.

Later on, William Aide asked me to turn pages when he recorded a piano concerto with the Toronto Symphony Orchestra. Once I turned the page too early and he whipped it back without missing a beat! I could have ruined the recording, and the entire orchestra would have had to start over from the beginning of the movement.

When I was in Grade 11, a girl in my class named Sharon invited me to the Sadie Hawkins dance. She was a talented pianist. Coached by my teacher, John, we won first place in a Kiwanis Festival duo-piano competition.

I was invited to dinner at Sharon's house. She had a beautiful grand piano and when she played, if she ever hit a wrong note, her father would shout, "*Mistake*," even if he was in another room. Her mother was studying painting, and on the living room wall was her portrait of Sharon. It was very accurate; except she'd painted her daughter with a considerably smaller nose. When Sharon saw me looking at the painting, she wasn't embarrassed at all. She laughed, enjoying the bizarre humour of it. I admired her character and wished I could be relaxed and spontaneous like her.

I was torn apart about what course to take in university. I wanted to study only one thing: piano. But the course in piano playing gave only a diploma, and I wanted a degree. The Bachelor of Music Program gave a degree, but it was a preparation for teaching music in high school. I had hated high school and certainly didn't want to be a high school teacher (a great irony, considering what happened later), so I applied for Honour Music, a preparation for graduate work in musicology.

During all my high school years, the only time I ever felt popular and accepted was at Geneva Park, a YMCA camp and conference centre, and it was largely because of my music. A distant relative was director, and I got hired on staff for the two summers after Grades 12 and 13. There was an upright piano in the boathouse and a grand piano in the conference centre, and both staff and cottagers really enjoyed my music.

In August 1963, I was at Geneva Park when I received my Grade 13 departmental exam results in the mail. The suspense of waiting for results of province-wide exams (which were the sole basis of admission to university) had been almost unbearable. We all got our mail at the same time, and I could hear girls screaming with excitement. To my immense relief, I had done well and would be accepted into Honour Music at the University of Toronto.

CHAPTER 8

University

I started Honour Music in September 1963. There were only about a dozen of us in the course. We were told that it was one of the heaviest courses at the University of Toronto. We took almost all of our courses with the students in the honour degree course in that particular discipline.

University was the first educational level I enjoyed. The professors were polite and treated us with respect. They didn't nag or bully us, as previous teachers had. Also, I loved the anonymity of a big university like the U of T. I didn't have to socialize or go to football games and could just focus on learning.

My courses were very demanding, and I also had to squeeze in piano practice to prepare for my ARCT exam. I worked almost all my waking hours and became a cerebral machine. I now realize that working all the time allowed me to avoid facing other people and the pain in my life.

At U of T, every first-year student had to take a Phys Ed course—sports or swimming. I chose swimming because I didn't like sports. Swimming took place in the pool at Hart House, a male bastion. All swimmers had to be nude. You were to complete a certain number of hours and fulfill certain requirements.

The life-saving session is the one I'll never forget. My partner was a handsome boy I had never met before. We were left alone in the pool to practise. I had to pretend I was drowning, and he had to rescue me, pull me out of the pool on my back, and then give me mouth-to-mouth resuscitation, which he did with no holding back. (At that time, I had no idea that there might be other people like me.) It would have been heaven; except I was hugely embarrassed because I was sure my excitement must be visible. Shortly after that, I went to see a C.S. practitioner but described my problem only as a "sexual dysfunction," never mentioning my attraction to boys.

Before Christmas we had a test in each academic course, with a mark assigned to let us know how we were doing. I remember the test in philosophy. It was one essay question, but I knew nothing about the topic. Terrified, I asserted Christian Science ideas about my mind being a reflection of God's mind. I calmed down and wrote anything I could think of relating to the topic. Most of the class failed, but I passed and came to the conclusion that university was an obstacle course to weed out the faint of heart. This observation and my success on the test gave me the courage to face the rest of the year's assignments and exams. At the end of the academic year when the results were published in the *Toronto Star*, I rushed to get a copy. When I opened the newspaper and saw the results, I couldn't believe it: I had come first in Honour Music!

Dad worked at the Ontario Department of Health, Christie Street Lab, near U of T, and suggested I get a ride home with him if my classes ended at the time he left the lab. I took him up on it once. When I arrived at the lab, Dad introduced me to another scientist. Her name was Glen, and she smiled a warm smile and said sincerely, "Your dad is so proud of you!" I thought, *How bizarre!* He never showed *me* that he was proud of me. In fact, he seldom even talked to me.

Dad regularly gave a young woman in his office a ride. Her name was Sally. I'd never met her, but one day, out of the blue, as if he had to share it with *someone* and I was the only one available at the time, Dad, with a salacious smile on his face, told me that she had "a boil on her bum."

Sally sat in the front passenger seat and I in the back. After Dad pulled into her driveway, they sat there whispering for five or ten minutes until she got out of the car. I was so hurt that he had so little regard for me that he would behave that way right in front of me. I wondered why he had even suggested I get a ride home with him. Needless to say, I never took him up on his offer again. However, one morning after that, Mother, my cousin, and I had to go downtown for some event so we got a ride with Dad. He picked up Sally, who refused to even speak to us. After Dad let the three of us off, my cousin said, "Isn't she strange! I think she's got a crush on Dick" (my father). I looked over apprehensively at my mother, but she showed no reaction.

While in university, I became more active in Christian Science. On Sundays I attended church with Mother. Christian Science services have no sermon, consisting only of a religious solo, three hymns, and readings from the Bible and the C.S. textbook, *Science and Health*. Only once did Dad attend the service with us. Unfortunately, the reading that ended the service on that occasion was: *"To happify existence by constant intercourse with those adapted to elevate it should be the motive of society."* When he heard these words, Dad jerked his head in disbelief, looking around the auditorium to see how others were reacting, but everyone, including Mother and I, looked straight ahead. I was ashamed of Christian Science and wondered why that particular quotation had been picked.

I also started attending the Forum (the C.S. young people's club) more frequently. During my four years at U of T, I also went to the weekly C.S. Org. services in a little chapel in Hart House, where I accompanied the hymns on a small antique organ that pumped air when you pedalled with both feet and swelled the music when you pushed your knees out.

One summer I went with a few other U of T "Org" members to the biennial meeting at the mother church in Boston. I stayed at MIT and still remember the man who received me saying sarcastically to his assistant, "Show the young *scientist* to his room." There were hundreds of students from many different countries there. We heard many talks and testimonies of healings through C.S., and the huge group got really pumped up.

I attended the Wednesday testimonial service at the mother church and witnessed something I'd never seen before at any of the many testimony meetings I'd attended in Toronto. The reader was a tall, senatorial-looking White man. A young Black man stood up and gave a testimony about a healing involving a knife wound. He spoke graphically and dramatically about the huge amount of blood he'd lost to convince us of what a miraculous healing it was. Christian Scientists tend to be White, very restrained people, who are engaged in a constant struggle to deny the physical, and you could feel the tension in the audience. The reader intervened once, asking the man to please focus on the *spiritual* meaning of the healing, but the young man didn't seem to realize that even though *he* was completely comfortable with this physical world, his audience was becoming apoplectic. With great sincerity, he continued describing the river of blood he'd witnessed. Finally, the reader interrupted him a second time, saying firmly, "Please bring your testimony to a conclusion!" I felt so sorry for the man who, not understanding C.S. culture, enthusiastically embraced his new faith but was mystified by the disapproval.

Seeing the C.S. practitioner when I was in first year hadn't helped me, and by third year I was so distressed about my sexual problems that I went to see a psychiatrist at the University Health Centre. I tried to explain what was bothering me without being too direct, never mentioning my attraction to males. At the end of the session, he shocked me by saying, "Well, our time is up. I assume you're in a religion like Christian Science. I notice you have a bleeding rash on your right hand. It must be really itchy to make you scratch it until it bleeds. It's called psychosomatic epidermidis and comes from nervous tension. You might want to get a prescription to help clear it up. Would you like to make an appointment for next week?" I said no and ran to my art history class with my mind racing, totally unable to concentrate on the slides the prof was showing. I felt so exposed, transparent. How could he know that I was a Christian Scientist? What else did he know that I hadn't even told him?

My friend Bruce from Geneva Park told me that he was going to Europe in the summer of 1966 through the German Club at York University, so I decided to join the German club at U of T and go as well. We had to work in Germany during June and July and then had August to tour Europe before our plane took us back to Canada. I realize how good Geneva Park was for me. It built my confidence and I met such great people. Bruce was handsome, intelligent, and popular, and he seemed to really like me. He went to Europe on a different flight, and his job was in a different part of Germany, but we had arranged to meet in Vienna in August.

At the beginning of the trip after arriving in Frankfurt, we had a week-long orientation in Germany. Every morning at six, a deep, masculine voice woke us up with a loud, "*Guten Morgen!*" One day we toured a castle. Another day we went to West Berlin, where I remember wishing that some boys in my group would stop shouting abuse at the armed East German soldiers in the patrol boats on the river. We crossed into East Berlin at one point, and I saw many bombed buildings and people with missing limbs.

I signed up for a job in Bavaria in the resort town of Bad Wiessee on a beautiful lake near the mountains, the most picturesque place I've ever seen. Once, a superb symphony orchestra from Munich came to the town and played Mozart symphonies in the open air.

I worked in a hotel dining room as a busboy, carrying beer mugs and dirty dishes and loading them into automatic dishwashers. I saw a side of life I'd never encountered before. One of my co-workers was an alcoholic and finished all the beer left in each mug before he put it in the dishwasher. One couple consisted of a man and a woman, and her face was twisted and distorted from being beaten by him.

I didn't like a lot of the food we were given, such as pig lung soup, so I ate a lot of stale rye bread. I slept in a basement room that was damp and airless. I got sick and feverish, and every morning I had to take my soaked bedding out to dry in the sun. A woman who worked there told me that I should go to the doctor and that health care was free in Germany. My reason for not going, of course, was my religion.

My German wasn't very good. The only person I could talk to was the receptionist, who spoke English, until an American high school student named Tom came on staff. His first words were, "Doesn't anybody here speak American?"

I remember telling the receptionist that Tom and I were going to visit Dachau concentration camp. She tried to get us not to go, but we went. It was horrifying to see the rooms where the Nazis gassed people and the ovens where they were burned, but I always wanted to know about reality, no matter how grim. One night we went to a bar in Munich to meet Tom's older brother. I knew Tom was a Catholic, and I had told him I was a Christian Scientist. Tom's brother got drunk and loud, and at a certain point, shouted something contemptuous that started with, "Well, my Christian Scientist friend …" He was quite hostile to me because of my religion.

I went once to a C.S. church in Munich. I was impressed that the same two readers did the service in German and then repeated it in English. A friendly man invited me to go back to his place and have Sunday dinner with his family. He was an English teacher and asked if he could have a look at my copy of *Europe on $5 A Day*. He seemed very amused to see the north of Germany dismissed as "grim and industrial."

In August I took the train to Vienna and met Bruce. He couldn't believe how much weight I'd lost from being sick. I had so much luggage that it was impossible to travel with it. He helped me ship a lot of it back to Toronto so I could travel more easily. We explored the spots in Vienna recommended in *Europe on $5 a Day*.

We went on to Italy, which I loved. In Venice we went on a gondola. Every morning was sunny and we'd go to a cafe and have a pastry and tea with lemon. In Florence I saw the art and architecture I'd studied. In Rome there was lots to see. The Sistine Chapel was a thrilling world of rust colours, as moving as a great piece of music. To save money we ate in the Vatican Cafeteria for the Poor, which served cheap but delicious food.

Bruce was tall and had a blond beard. I remember a woman seeing him and exclaiming, "Il vero Cristo!" ("The true Christ!")

We arrived in Barcelona in the middle of the night and were trying to sleep on the benches in the train station when a cab driver took pity on us and drove us to his place. He led us to a room with a single bed, told us to be quiet and not wake his wife and kids, and headed back to work. I had to spend six hours in a single bed with a handsome boy! I didn't sleep a wink. At 6:00 a.m. the kind cab driver arrived and took us to the area where we wanted to stay. Later we ran into a girl we'd met on the train previously, who said to me, "What's wrong? You look like the cat who swallowed the canary."

In Barcelona we saw a bullfight. It was so cruel! I wondered how the spectators could stand to see the bull repeatedly jabbed until it finally fell down. Machines arrived to clean up the blood so they could bring in another poor beast to slaughter. I felt I had to go to one bullfight to see what it was like, but I would never go again.

From Barcelona we went to Sitges, a resort town on the Spanish Riviera, where we swam and lay on the beach for a couple of days then headed to Paris. Bruce was getting tired of museums and art galleries, but I had to see the Louvre and other tourist destinations. We looked up the parents of a friend of John Leberg, who had us to dinner. I remember playing "Autumn Leaves" on their piano while they hummed along.

Once Bruce and I had lunch in a park in Paris. We had a bottle of wine and some bread and cheese. In no time Bruce had consumed almost everything, and I got only a small fraction of the meal. I should have said something, even in a joking way, but I didn't know how to communicate my needs. (Decades later, I'm still working on being assertive, but I have made some progress.)

Paris was our last stop before it was time to separate. Bruce went to Germany, and I went to London, where I had three days until my flight left for Toronto. I stayed in the YMCA. Huge English breakfasts came with the room, so I gorged myself and started putting weight back on. I saw Buckingham Palace, Saint Paul's, and Westminster Abbey before flying back to Toronto for my final year of Honour Music.

One weekend in the spring of 1967, I was lucky enough to go to the Montreal World's Fair with the Forum and stay in Habitat, that famous structure that looked like a bunch of blocks piled irregularly on each other.

That summer, I picked up my girlfriend, Sarah, and we drove to visit her grandparents at their cottage. We then headed to my parents' cottage on Twelve-Mile Bay, where Mom and Dad were going to join us later in the day. I needed to buy something and saw a store on the left side of the highway. I slowed down and started turning left. A car raced past me just as I was turning, and the driver swerved to avoid hitting me and went off the road and into the boulders below.

Sarah went into the store to call 911, and I ran down to see if I could help. I'll never forget the scene down there. The car had been abruptly stopped by the boulders. One wheel was still spinning. Inside, the driver was sitting behind the steering wheel in shock, and the woman in the passenger seat was moaning: "Oh my God! Oh my God!" Her head had smashed the windshield. A little piece of skin hung down from the glass, and I heard what sounded like rain. It was blood from her forehead dripping onto some plastic. The police arrived and took our information, and the ambulance attendants put the couple on stretchers and raced to the hospital. Dad's car was hardly damaged, so we drove to the cottage.

Throughout the whole incident I was completely cerebral. I silently made C.S. affirmations but couldn't help thinking, *This isn't supposed to happen to a Christian Scientist.* When my parents arrived, I waited quite a while before I calmly told them what had happened. They had no reaction. To this day I've never faced up to the traumatic horror and guilt of the accident. Ever since then, whenever I'm travelling on a highway, I experience great fear of an accident, and I'm so relieved when I arrive at my destination safely.

CHAPTER 9

New Directions

In the spring of 1967, I completed my B.A. in Honour Music. My hard work had paid off: I scored in the eighty-ninth percentile on my Graduate Record Exam. I had applied to seven universities and was accepted into a master's program in musicology at four of them. I was agonizing over which one to choose when, out of the blue, Dad said, "I think you should get some work experience before you continue your education." I had put so much effort into this next step in my education—applying to universities, writing letters, paying application fees—but for some reason I conceded to him and considered what job I could do to make money for graduate school. My cousin's husband had become a high school teacher, the last thing I wanted to do, but it would just be a year or two until I'd saved enough money for graduate school, so I called him and got some information about teaching high school in Toronto.

Normally you had to have a one-year Bachelor of Education degree in order to qualify to teach. However, there was such a demand for teachers at the time that a special one-month summer course, followed by a paid probationary year of teaching and then a second summer course, had been set up. By the time I decided to go this route, it was the last week you could apply. To get into the course you had to have already been hired for a teaching job. There were two music jobs left in Toronto, so I interviewed for both. Both were in tech schools—not where I wanted to be, especially for music. The first interview involved a principal with a "Why do you think we'd want to hire you?" approach.

My second interview was with a very welcoming principal. I had applied for the job teaching band—not what I wanted, but the only subject I was technically qualified to teach. The principal asked me about my musical background. When I told him I played piano, he said, "Well, I do have another job that just opened up this morning. It consists of teaching Grade 13 music at 8:00 a.m., playing organ four mornings a week for assemblies, and teaching English for the rest of the timetable." I said I would prefer that timetable.

He took me down to the auditorium to see the organ. It was a beautiful Casavant pipe organ like the one at First Church. He asked me if I thought I could play it, and I said I could probably manage. We went back to his office and he told me what English classes I'd be teaching. That evening I went to his house and signed a contract (no turning back now). My salary was to be $6,400 a year. It seemed like a lot to me at the time. In a couple of years, I'd have enough money for graduate school.

When I told my friends in the Forum that I'd be teaching at Central Tech, they were surprised I'd take a job in such a "tough" school, which made me very apprehensive.

The following week I started my teacher's course. There were hundreds of students. A principal who spoke to us said he was so desperate for teachers that he'd take anyone "alive and breathing." Overall, the courses weren't great, but my English professor was very good. I remember that once he got us to close our eyes and try to write some dictated words, explaining this as a way to prepare students for studying Milton's "On His Blindness."

I began teaching at Central Tech the day after Labour Day. My friends were right. It was a tough school! The student body consisted almost entirely of boys, and sixty per cent of them were in non-academic programs. Every classroom had desks with "Black Power" scrawled on them and sunflower seed shells inside of them (although I never once saw a student eating sunflower seeds). The school had over three thousand students, even though it wasn't built for nearly that number. Classes were squeezed into every available space. I was very nervous, but luckily I taught my English classes in what was previously a science lab, standing behind a high counter so the students couldn't see my knees knocking together.

On the Friday evening after my first week teaching, I went to see *To Sir with Love* and was overcome with emotion. Shivers ran up and down my spine from seeing the same kind of emotionally-charged, disadvantaged, needy students in a melodramatic relationship with their teacher that I had just experienced.

My daily routine was: teach music at 8:00 a.m., play the organ at 9:00, then teach English until 3:15. Later in the year I worked after school as vocal coach for the school musicals, occasionally as late as 10:00 p.m.

I had started teaching high school without any practice-teaching experience whatsoever. My department head was officially assigned to help me, but I didn't learn much from him. I was lucky to find an unofficial mentor in Yvonne, one of the more than thirty new teachers who flooded into Central Tech that September. She was thirteen years older than me and had taught elementary school before switching to high school. She was a superb teacher, and I learned so much from her. Also, I was concerned about whether, as an introvert, I could be an effective teacher, but she maintained that someone who could sit alone and plan lessons had an advantage in teaching, which encouraged me.

One of my classes was Grade 12 English for students in the special art course. I was twenty-two. The students were all seventeen or eighteen, except for Andrew, who was forty. He didn't say much, but early in the course he raised his hand when the word "atheist" came up, and he coyly asked, "What's the difference between an *atheist* and an *agnostic*?" All eyes darted to him then back to me. Would I be able to meet the challenge and prove myself? I took a deep breath and said, "Good question!" I then calmly printed both words on the board and explained the difference. But then I also printed "believer" on the board and delivered an exhaustive explanation of the distinctions in meaning among the three words. Soon the students started looking bored again and the drama was over. My status in the classroom was maintained. *Whew*!

More challenging was my Grade 10 English class for students in the auto mechanics course. Some of them couldn't be intimidated by threats about losing marks, failing, or getting detentions. If I gave a detention, they didn't come to it, and if they got suspended, they didn't have to come to school at all. One day a boy named Doug told me to "F_ _ _ off!" I lost it and marched him down to the office. Yvonne, who'd heard me yelling, took over the class. Doug never came back. A couple of months later, I saw him coming toward me on Bloor Street. I was nervous (would he attack me?), but he said, "Hi, sir." When

I asked him how he was doing, he said he was working and that he'd been a "jerk" in school. I realized that some of these non-academic students had short fuses, but after they blew up, they often moved on (unlike a repressed person like me, who holds on to hurts forever).

To my surprise, the most difficult English class I had was a class of *girls*! They were in the Grade 10 home economics course. In one vicious fight, a large girl picked up a desk and threw it at another girl. And one girl pulled out another girl's hair by the roots and left the hair and a small section of scalp in the waste basket.

I did much better with academic classes because the students were motivated to learn, and they appreciated my hyper-organization and "We don't have a minute to waste" approach. I wasn't authoritarian, so I had to get control in other ways. Students would arrive for their forty-minute period talking and laughing, and I'd have to yell them down in order to start the lesson. I soon figured out a solution: I put the numbers for the homework on the board beforehand and asked each arriving student to put one answer on the board. I never stopped thinking about and refining my teaching techniques. "Trial and error" was my substitute for teacher-training.

When I started teaching, I was very naive. I loved my academic students, and it never occurred to me that they might cheat on tests. My brother Bob was in high school at the time, and when he heard that I'd assigned a poem for my students to write out by memory, he said that they would write out the poem beforehand, write some words on the piece of paper I had given out, and then pass in the prewritten poem when I came to collect the poems. I was sure he was wrong, but I put a tiny red dot on the back of each sheet of foolscap I gave out and, sure enough, three of the poems I collected had no red dot on the back!

Another cheater I caught had copied *Coles Notes* in the tiniest writing I've ever seen and taped them to his thin plastic ruler, which he slid out from under his sleeve to copy from during a test.

I was also naive about sexuality, having had almost no experience with either females or males. Sensing my naivety, one of the boys in my Grade 12 auto mechanics class tried to embarrass me by asking, "Hey, sir, Mr. P. says sex is no good the first time. Is that true?" I could feel my face getting red as I tried to figure out a response, but I didn't know what to say. After a few moments I awkwardly switched back to what I had been teaching.

For Christmas 1967, I was invited to go to Winnipeg. I went with my cousin who worked in Toronto and was going to visit her parents, my Aunt Margaret and Uncle Bob, and her brother, Bill. I stayed at Granny's apartment. We had a Christmas Eve celebration and a Christmas dinner at Aunt Margaret's.

I had a great visit with Granny at her place. She was eighty-five but still independent. We talked a lot about Christian Science. I told her that I was lucky that I had inherited Christian Science from her and Mother. Unfortunately, that comment impelled her to confide in me. She said, "Gus [her husband] never touched me. Your mother was the result of a virgin birth." Cringing inwardly, I struggled to look accepting and calm.

In July 1968, I took the second part of the teacher's course, and in August I took Class Instruction in Christian Science, which lasted two weeks and allowed me to style myself "Grant Reynolds, C.S." (not that I ever did). I joined the mother church in Boston and Fifth Church in Toronto.

Teaching resumed in September. It was still incredibly difficult but a little less stressful in that I had an idea of what to expect. However, I again had a Grade 10 English class of auto mechanics, this time with a student named Carlos, who always had an angry, ugly look on his face. One day he viciously attacked another student in my class. I got in between the two of them and held Carlos back. (My right arm hurt for a week.) The next year his Grade 11 English teacher told me that Carlos was in and out of court all the time for extorting money from homosexuals. Ten years later, I read that he was killed in a gangland slaying.

For the Christmas holiday, 1968, I registered to go skiing at Blue Mountain with the Forum. As it got closer to the holiday, more and more people dropped out until there were only two of us left: a girl named Jocelyn and me, but we decided that we would still go. She was an elementary teacher with whom I'd always enjoyed talking because she was warm and expressive with a good sense of humour. We had both started teaching in 1967 and had given a dual presentation to the Forum about teaching. I found her emphasis on using her pointer to discipline her little Grade 2 students off-putting, but otherwise she seemed to have a positive attitude toward teaching.

We stayed at The Lodge at Blue Mountain, which had separate quarters for men and women. Most of each day we spent skiing and going up the chairlifts. Joc introduced me to chocolate bars, which we often ate on the chairlift. Before this trip I didn't know the difference between a Coffee Crisp and a Mars bar, but she was familiar with every kind of chocolate bar, and soon so was I. In the evening we sat by the fire and talked, often including others (Joc was very sociable).

In January we returned to our respective schools. Joc taught at King Edward Public School, two blocks away from Central Technical School, where I taught, and she would often come to CTS after school and sit in the auditorium while I coached students singing in our current musical. Afterwards we would go to dinner at a nearby restaurant.

Joc was very easy to talk to, and we started confiding in each other about our lives. Both of her parents were Christian Scientists, and she told me they forced it on their children. Joc told me she didn't "get" the religion. (I had noticed that she would alienate others in the Forum by saying "unacceptable" things, such as her statement that she took wake-up pills when studying for exams.) Years later she told me she had hoped she might learn what was good about the religion from me. She told me her family lived in Etobicoke, but for a while she had lived downtown, close to where she taught. However, her mother had called her every day to get her to come back home to live, and finally she'd yielded.

Joc complained about her father. She told me about an incident that deeply moved me. As a child she had started putting on weight, and on one occasion when she recalled something that showed what a good memory she had, her father exclaimed, "Why, you're getting more like an elephant every day!" A very bright and sensitive child, she understood his double meaning immediately, and I could see how hurt she was. My heart went out to her, and I identified with her because I felt a similar pain in my own life.

She also told me that her father was violent and that once when she was doing dishes, he came toward her to hit her, and she warned him that if he came any closer, she'd break all the china dishes she was washing. When he did come closer, she lifted a pile of dishes in the air and smashed them on the floor, which shocked him into not touching her.

Another story that moved me involved both of her parents. She told me that when she was a teenager, she'd experienced a sharp pain in her abdomen. Every day it got worse, but her mother said she should just "know the truth" (Christian Science jargon for asserting that sickness wasn't real) instead of making a reality of the pain. When she got so sick that all she could do was lie in bed moaning, her mother still did nothing, but when her father came home from work and saw how sick she was, he carried her out to the car and raced to the hospital. The doctors performed surgery to save her life. It turned out she had appendicitis, which, because it wasn't treated, had caused peritonitis, and she had been close to death. When her mother came to the hospital after her surgery, Joc got emotional and burst out crying. Her mother said, "Well, if that's the way you're going to act, I'm leaving," and she walked out.

I felt such empathy for Joc. I think what brought us together was our hunger for the love and approval of our parents, which was so lacking.

Joc confided that at twelve, she had been sexually assaulted by a man who was an older distant relative. Ashamed, she had told no one about it. I told her about my attraction to males, and she seemed sympathetic, telling me about a man on her staff who everyone thought was gay. She liked him and was angry when people made fun of him behind his back.

Joc was the only person I'd ever told about my attraction to men. I felt such relief after all my years of secrecy, and I absolutely trusted her with my secret. One evening she called me at home to tell me there was a debate on TV about homosexuality. I had never seen the topic out in the open before. It had never occurred to me that anyone would even consider homosexuality "acceptable," as the people on one side of the debate did. It was the first time I'd ever seen two men holding hands! I remembered a Shakespeare quotation (familiar to me ironically because it is used at the beginning of "Science and Health"): "Nothing is good or bad but thinking maketh it so." I then saw it in a new light. *Perhaps it could be applied to everything, including sexuality,* I thought. That quote gave me the clear and liberating insight that homosexuality was neither good nor bad but just *was.*

Not long after this, I was with Joc at a meeting at Fifth Church listening to someone speak. Suddenly I had the clear realization that C.S. was just make-believe. All the talk about healing, but I'd never seen a single instance of it. I whispered to Joc, "Let's go." I walked out of the church and never went back. I withdrew from my Class Instruction Association, the mother church, and Fifth Church, Toronto. I had such a feeling of liberation and a new, good feeling toward others! However, with time, I also felt some sadness over leaving C.S. because in so doing, I was also separating myself from friends and family and hurting people I loved, like Granny.

Soon my two years of teaching to make money for graduate school were up, but I kept on putting off graduate school. After I took my third summer course and got my Specialist Certificate in Vocal Music, the principal said he wanted me to be Head of Music. I didn't want to teach band because most of the students would be at a very basic level, and I wouldn't have found it interesting or satisfying. I asked Yvonne what I should do. She gave me the best advice: "Be positive. Tell him you've been taking courses to get your specialist in English because English is the subject you want to teach." I did, and he seemed fine with that.

After two years the organist I had replaced came back to CTS and took over playing the organ at assemblies again. However, he often didn't show up, and I would have to leave my first-period English class at the last minute to cover for him. This really weakened my effectiveness with the class. I should have asked

Yvonne for advice, but I didn't. I went to the principal and said I didn't want to leave my class and cover for the organist anymore.

In the spring we got our timetables for the following year. All the other English teachers had thirty periods to teach. I had thirty-two, and my classroom was changed to a room in the basement with no windows. I went to the board personnel office and talked to the manager of personnel. I thought my department head was responsible, but Yvonne found out it was the principal who had ordered the timetable change! I realized then that it was payback for my refusal to continue leaving my class to cover for the organist.

I took English courses at night school and every summer to get my Specialist Certificate in English, qualifying me to teach Grade 13. It was hard work, but I loved teaching the academic, university-bound students.

CHAPTER 10

"A Tricky Business"

Joc and I continued to spend a lot of time together, and our friendship developed. We seemed to have goals in common. Like me, she wanted to extend her education. She had only finished Grade 12 and Teachers College but told me she wanted to get a university degree. She said her family had made it difficult for her to succeed in school.

I still had keys to the building where the Forum met, and one night we went inside and I asked Joc if I could try having sex with her. I had told her about my attraction to men but not about my inability to masturbate. There was no foreplay. She just allowed me to penetrate her. It felt great and I had orgasm, withdrawing just in time. I was surprised and relieved that I could function sexually.

One cold winter night in 1969, after we'd been out, I brought her back to her parents' house. It was late and everyone seemed to have gone to bed. We sat in the living room talking quietly, at one point casually speculating about getting a place together. Her sister, who was eavesdropping, woke her mother to tell her we had plans to live together, and her mother came downstairs in her nightgown and read what Mary Baker Eddy says about marriage. I said I didn't believe in C.S. anymore and left. The next day all of Joc's furniture was put out on the front lawn and she was told to find somewhere else to live. I felt she had become *my* responsibility.

We found a basement apartment for Joc near her school in a house owned by a Portuguese man who seemed nice. However, soon Joc suspected him of creeping around the basement and spying on her. She got more and more upset over the next couple of months. I suggested she get a self-contained apartment. During the March Break, we rented separate apartments in the same High Park high-rise. My idea was that we'd be close by to support each other in our new lives but be relatively independent. However, Joc never furnished or lived in her apartment.

She started taking birth control pills. We had sex regularly, and it continued to be great for me. I could never get enough. Once Joc got very playful and actually succeeded in masturbating me! It was wonderfully liberating. I never had trouble masturbating again and suspect that my previous "deficiency" was caused by my Puritan religion and attraction to men, (which was still there but seemed to be reduced).

Living together without being married was fairly rare at the time and unacceptable to many. Joc's family refused to see us except for one invitation when her mother had a woman from church over to tell us about *her* daughter "shacking up" with a man and what a bad idea it was.

One evening the buzzer rang and it was my sixteen-year-old brother. He wanted to come up and see my new "pad." Joc dashed into the coat closet just before he arrived with a couple of his friends. I nervously showed them around the apartment and we chatted for a while. Although it seemed forever, they didn't stay very long. As he went out the door, my brother said loudly, "Good night, Joc!"

Joc was always short of money and I found out why; she had many high-interest charge accounts. For example, she had bought a set of encyclopedias with payments spread over many years. Naive as I was, I thought that she just didn't understand money and explained to her that by financing her purchase over many years, she would be paying three times the cost of the set. I paid off the set myself, realizing later that, intelligent as she was, she understood basic finance but just didn't want to be restricted.

As time went on, Joc and I had more and more disagreements. I had no one to get advice from, so I looked up Dr. Moore, the psychiatrist I'd seen once at U of T, and started seeing him weekly. I told him that, to my surprise, sex with a woman was great, and I certainly had no trouble performing as I had always feared, but I still had an attraction to men.

One evening Joc told me that her mother had called and said that everyone at church was talking about our living together. She told me her mother had broken down crying and said the stress was affecting her heart. I didn't propose, but stupidly said, "Well, maybe we should consider marriage."

When I told Dr. Moore about the situation, he said, "I would wait. Marriage is a tricky business at the best of times." When I came back and told Joc what he'd said, she slumped down in her chair and her eyes rolled back into her head in what she had once described as "a catatonic state." It was really scary. I'd never seen anything like it before. I felt she might commit suicide. I decided I had to marry her.

When we told her mother we were getting married, she was thrilled and rushed over and threw her arms around me. Since I was now an atheist, I wanted a *civil* wedding. My future mother-in-law quipped, "Well, a *civil* wedding is better than I ever had." We got an appointment at City Hall for August 20, 1969.

When we told my father we were getting married, he said sarcastically, "Aren't you having *enough* fun?"

Joc's parents had my parents and us to dinner. Before dinner we sat in the living room. Joc's father, a smooth-talking salesman, kept trying to get a conversation going, but my parents never picked up on any of his many leads. They just sat there expressionless. I was so embarrassed. Dad looked very uncomfortable and even hostile (as he had with the woman in the tuck shop at Jimmy's cottage). My two years of teaching had made me a little better at socializing, so I joined in to try to help Joc's father, but it was a painful evening.

Joc's parents also started having Joc and me to dinner before we got married. At that time Joc's younger sister and two younger brothers lived there, all high school students. Joc's family was so different from my quiet, uncommunicative one. There was so much arguing, joking, and fast talk that I could barely eat my meal because I was so tense. I felt like they were the noisy Jewish family and I was the quiet Anglo-Saxon date in a Woody Allen film. There was a lot of teasing, which could change to anger in a flash! Once Joc's father brought a book about wedding customs to the table and started reading it, incorporating comments about our coming wedding. I didn't see his kidding as nasty, but Joc got up from the table and said, "I'm leaving!" Looking at me, she added, "If you want to come, you'd better hurry." I hesitated, too stunned to react, and she left in the car without me. It took me hours to walk from Etobicoke to High Park, where we lived. When I got there, I was too furious to go up to the apartment. I had my own set of car keys and went into the underground parking and tried to sleep in the car, but after a couple of uncomfortable hours, I went up to the apartment.

As the date for the wedding approached, I felt more and more resistance to getting married. I told Joc I needed to try having sex with a man. We lived near High Park, so it was easy to find one. We went up to Joc's unoccupied apartment, but when I saw him in the light, I found him unattractive, and we didn't have sex.

The day before the wedding, we sublet Joc's apartment to a young woman who was an elementary teacher like Joc. After we showed her the apartment, Joc had her down to our apartment for tea. Joc was very friendly to her, and I tried to be too, even though I would have been brief and business-like if it were just me. After the woman left, Joc had a major temper tantrum, accusing me of flirting with the woman. I told her I was just trying to imitate her sociable approach. The more I explained this, the more furious Joc became. This was our worst fight ever, and I debated calling the wedding off, but because it was to take place the next day, I felt I couldn't.

Our parents and two grandmothers joined us for the wedding at City Hall the next day. We all waited until we heard the clerk yell, "Reynolds." We went into a room, had five or ten minutes of wedding formula from the judge, then vacated the room for the next couple. Joc's father extended his hand and said sincerely, "Welcome to the family."

Admittedly, the wedding had been very business-like and impersonal, but still I thought it cruel that Joc's grandmother had to say, "That was the only wedding I've ever been to that I didn't cry at."

I had wanted to go somewhere special for our honeymoon, to stay in a fancy hotel and be served our meals in a nice dining room, but Joc insisted on going to my parents' cottage. As usual, I gave in. We had to carry water up from the lake, drive into town and buy groceries, transport them across the lake, and then cook our meals on a hotplate. The cottage was only accessible by water, and I always felt totally trapped there. You couldn't even go for a walk! Unlike me, Joc liked socializing and had people over for dinner: my aunt and uncle (who had a cottage farther down the bay), and then a strange man a few cottages down, with whom she had a heated argument during dinner about which supermarket had the lowest prices.

When we got back to Toronto, we had to go to a reception my mother had arranged for her female friends and relatives to meet my new wife. When Audrey met her, she told Joc how wonderful I was. When we got home, Joc exploded in rage. How dare Audrey say nice things about the groom! It was the *bride* who was to be praised! *But,* I thought to myself, *Audrey doesn't know Joc, so how can she praise her?*

In September we returned to teaching. I realized my plan to work for just a year or two to finance graduate school was fading. This would be my *third* year of teaching.

Joc announced that she wanted to be a social worker someday and needed to work with older students, but her principal kept her teaching lower grades. One day in November, she came home from work to tell me that she had resigned, effective January! What a shock! She'd never once mentioned the possibility of retiring.

When January came, she had nothing to do, so she would drive to the school, pick me up, drive me home for lunch, and then race me back to school. The lunch period was only forty-five minutes, and the third time we did this, I was late getting back. A VP had unlocked my classroom door and was waiting for me with the students. Humiliated, I apologized. In my two years of teaching, I'd never been late before. I told Joc that evening I was never going to come home for lunch again.

Joc didn't have enough high school credits to get into university, so she enrolled in a pre-university English course for mature students. She did well, getting accepted into York University for the following September.

In the summer of 1970, we drove out West, sleeping in a little tent at night. Joc did most of the driving. If I asked her to stop so that I could get an ice cream cone, she'd yell *"Hurry!"* from the car. I'd have to jump in the car so she could keep ahead of a particular transport truck she had finally passed ten minutes before. I soon decided the ice cream cone wasn't worth the tension around stopping and never asked again.

We drove to Thunder Bay, where she'd grown up, and I met her relatives. Despite her apparent warmth to them, Joc was sometimes negative about them. After a very warm goodbye to one cousin, she told me she suspected her of stealing her hairbrush.

We headed west. In Winnipeg we were walking along the sidewalk one day when Joc started screaming abuse at me, calling me a "fucking homosexual!" I still remember the shocked, mortified look on the face of the man who witnessed this.

Our ultimate destination was Calgary, where her oldest brother lived. We went to the Calgary Stampede with him and his wife. Even though it was ninety degrees, I was comfortable. I liked the dry air of Calgary so much that I later applied to teach there, but the Alberta Department of Education said my qualifications were below the minimum required, even though they were as high as you could get in Ontario. I'm glad now that I was rejected because later a White teacher at my school told me that he and his Black wife had experienced a lot of racism in Calgary and were glad to have moved to Toronto.

We seemed to be having a good visit, but after a few days, Joc had an argument with her brother. It was behind closed doors, so his wife and I couldn't hear what they were saying. Joc emerged very upset and got more and more angry. Her brother's wife asked me if I knew why Joc "had a bee in her bonnet." I told her I didn't.

We left abruptly. Joc wouldn't say what was wrong. I'd never seen her so sad, and I assumed it was because of my attraction to men. When we found a camping spot, I was overwhelmed with grief that I had hurt her so much. While she was busy, I walked away and for the first time in my life attempted suicide. I jumped into a river and tried for a long time to drown myself by staying under water, but I couldn't make it happen. Joc contacted a park ranger. When they found me, he said we had to leave the park. I never told her why I wanted to die, nor did she tell me what had made her so sad, but I realized I could never again allow myself to try to enter the dark places in her mind.

In May 1971, Joc announced that she was pregnant. I was not pleased! Although never discussing it with me, she had stopped taking her birth control pills, claiming her psychiatrist thought fatherhood would be good for me, and she hadn't thought she could *actually* get pregnant. After my horrible childhood, I certainly never wanted to be a father, sure that I'd be a cold, ugly failure like my own father. When people congratulated me, I couldn't smile.

Joc continued to take control of everything. Our lease was coming up, and she thought the apartment we had was too expensive, so she found a second-floor flat in a house. It was a disaster! I could no longer play my piano because it had to be stored in a room downstairs, to which I had no access. In summer, the apartment was insufferably hot, the hottest place I've ever lived in my whole life! There was no door at the top of the stairs, just a curtain, and Joc thought the old man who lived below us was always standing silently behind this curtain.

In July we went West again, this time stopping in Winnipeg to visit my Aunt Margaret, Uncle Bob, Cousin Bill, and Granny. Bill was excited to show us his new cottage. We arrived there to find a very rustic, spider-infested shack. Joc, pregnant and very irritable, was openly angry at being taken there. Bill was disappointed and Joc was furious at everyone except Granny. I remember my aunt pressing a folded twenty-dollar bill into Joc's hand to try to comfort her as we left for points farther west. The Rockies were beautiful, but I was glad to get home, having had more than enough camping for a lifetime.

CHAPTER 11

Children

Over time, I had adjusted to the reality that I was going to be a father. I hoped for a boy, feeling that somehow I'd be able to reverse the negative relationship I'd had with my own father. And on November 7, 1971, my son was born. When I first held Stephen, I was overwhelmed with joy and love.

Joc had said she wanted to have children so she could "lavish love upon them." At the time that statement seemed over the top, but it turned out to be true. She never stopped interacting with Steve, smiling at him, and expressing her love. It was a beautiful thing to watch.

Our landlady had told us our rent was just $140 a month, but we had blown a fuse the first weekend after we moved in so she insisted we pay for our electricity. Now she demanded extra money for water because of the baby. Joc's mother visited and the idea of buying a house came up. I remember her encouraging smile as she said, "I think with your salary you could afford it."

We looked at houses in Toronto, but they were too expensive. Eventually we found a small, detached house in Mississauga near the Credit Valley that we could afford, but I had no down payment. Mother arranged a loan for us, even though I never asked her to. It was a great help, but after all the financial arrangements were concluded, her last words as we left were, "Don't blame me if the house doesn't work out."

The contrast was so very clear. My mother-in-law had made me feel good about this venture just through her smile and encouraging words, but my mother, though she had done the work to make the purchase of the house possible, had left me feeling negative about it (and about her).

Steve was about six months old when we moved into the new house. I couldn't wait to come home and play with him every day. I remember Joc grabbing one of his legs and saying, "He's *my* baby!" I'd grab the other and say, "No, he's *my* baby!" Each of us would gently pull one of his legs. Steve laughed his head off (and so did we). I'd never guessed that a child could bring such joy … I suppose because my parents had never shown joy in me.

They say you never love a house as much as your first one. Joc put floor to ceiling mirrors on the upstairs wall, got new broadloom, and made other improvements. I painted the house inside and outside and built a fence around the back yard. This was the happiest time Joc and I ever had.

Before Steve was two, Joc got pregnant again. This time I was in the room for the birth. I wanted only two children. I already had a boy, and I was so anxious that this one be a girl that when the baby finally came out and it *was* a girl, I fainted for the first time in my life. Julie was born on March 27, 1974. I now had "a millionaire's family!"

With two children to look after, Joc became much more anxious and upset than previously. She arrived home from the doctor's one day looking like she was going to cry. When I asked what was wrong, she was reluctant to say, but when I pursued it, she blurted out angrily that the doctor had spent too long examining her breasts. She then immediately shifted all of that anger toward me. She could never admit what she was feeling or allow herself to be comforted. From then on, she was often angry at me, and we fought a lot of the time. There didn't have to be any reason for the anger.

I'd been seeing Dr. Moore individually, but he put me in a group of men who weren't necessarily gay but "insecure about their masculinity." Joc was totally opposed to it. She thought it wasn't efficient therapy, and I wondered myself. (In retrospect, I realize the group experience was something I needed because I was so uncomfortable with men.) I stopped going and found another psychiatrist.

After a few sessions, my new psychiatrist told me he thought aversive therapy might help me, so he referred me to the Clarke Institute (now called CAMH). When I arrived there, a receptionist told me to have a seat in the waiting room. Eventually, a very short, middle-aged man with Coke-bottle eyeglasses and a heavy German accent came out, announced that he was Dr. Franck, and invited me into his office. When he asked me why I was there, I told him I was married to a woman but was attracted to men, and my psychiatrist thought I might be able to be cured through shock therapy. He said, "No! Is not possible. I am expert on homosexuality. There is no cure. You got married *und* now you must get unmarried." I left totally discouraged.

Soon I found yet another psychiatrist. His name was Dr. Lamon. Unlike all the other psychiatrists I'd seen, he listened attentively as I described my problems, and he displayed real empathy.

Joc's abuse got worse, so one Sunday I decided to leave. I called my brother to see if I could stay at his place, and then I packed my car. Joc had tried to distract Stephen's attention from my departure, and my last view was of him spraying Windex on the sliding glass doors and wiping them vigorously. This was one of the saddest moments of my entire life. I couldn't bear to leave three-year-old Steve and baby Julie, but I made myself drive off. I didn't sleep a wink that night, haunted by the image of Steve wiping the windows.

In the morning my brother went to work, but I was so tired and upset, I called in sick. For hours I just stared out the window, missing Steve and Julie so much. Finally, I could stand it no longer and put everything back in my car, wrote a note to my brother to thank him for his hospitality, and headed home. Joc was feeding the kids when I arrived. I told her I wanted to come back. I sat at the table staring at my beautiful children, at peace now that I was back with them.

The next time I saw Dr. Lamon, I blubbered like a baby about how people *say* they stay together for the sake of their children, but it's really for their own sake because they can't bear not to be with them.

I saw Dr. Lamon for a year or so before I felt I could move on. When I told him I was leaving, he said, "I'm sorry." When I asked him why, he thought for a bit and then said, "Because most of my patients either blame themselves entirely or others entirely for all their problems, but you strike a perfect balance between blaming yourself and blaming others."

I enjoyed my children so much. Julie's babytalk was so cute! Every once in a while, Joc would get frustrated and shout, "I want privacy!" One day when Joc came into her room, two-year-old Julie asserted, "I want *puffy!*"

After she learned to walk, Julie would wait for me to come home from work every day, and we'd join hands and go for a tour of the back yard. If it was warm, we'd walk through the grass in our bare feet. It was a ritual we both loved. Joc said that Julie was "the apple of my eye," and it was true. Once at the dinner table, turning to Joc, Julie announced, "When I grow up, I want to marry Daddy." I was relieved that nobody laughed at her, and that with a warm smile and gentle tone of voice, Joc replied, "That's nice, honey, but you can't because I'm already married to him."

From her earliest days, Julie had a strong sense of justice. At the age of three, after being spanked by her mother, she calmly announced, "When I grow up and *you're* little, I'm going to spank you, too." She thought that just as she was little and growing bigger, grown-ups would go in the opposite direction and grow smaller.

Steve started kindergarten and learned some new vocabulary. When Joc came toward him to punish him, he warned her: "If you come any closer, I'll say the word with the *fuh* and the *uh* and the *kuh*!" She couldn't spank him that time because she was laughing so hard. But she often did spank him, and he became quite defiant when she threatened to, once even saying, "Go ahead. I like a little pain!"

Later Steve started stealing all the change we left around. I found it very distressing and told him that nobody liked someone they couldn't trust. I had read Rudolf Dreikurs' *Discipline without Tears* and tried one of his approaches with Steve, explaining that everybody does bad things sometimes, but just because you do a bad thing, it doesn't mean you're a bad person. Steve paused to think about what I'd said, then he repeated, "So just because I do a bad thing, it doesn't mean I'm a bad person." A look of great relief came over his face. He smiled a big smile and never stole money again.

Our new house was quite far away from Central Tech, and I had complained from time to time about the long trip to and from work. Joc surprised me one day by suggesting we sell it and move closer to Toronto. We listed it, but when it sold, she burst out crying and accused *me* of selling her house. I had assumed that Joc had contacted the real estate agent, but I later found out the agent had knocked on the door one day and charmed Joc into putting the house up for sale. Even though her father was a salesman, Joc was often manipulated by salespeople and seemed unaware of what they were up to.

When the closing date arrived, we discovered that the agent had changed the offer to purchase so that we would have to pay much more than the original offer we had signed. I steeled myself and called the head of the real estate company at his home and told him of this. He replied in a booming voice, "Mr. Reynolds, I'm a rich man, and I don't need your money. If what you say is true, heads will roll!" He replaced the agent with another and had the offer changed back to the original.

Joc seemed to become more troubled after we moved to the new house. She thought a boy was breaking branches off the trees in our front yard, bought a spotlight, and would lie underneath the bay window with it all night to catch the culprit, but never succeeded in doing so.

I worried about the kids' safety. One day Joc remembered she needed something from the supermarket and left three-year-old Julie having a bath while she went to get it. When she got back she went upstairs and there naked in the tub with Julie was her four-year-old friend, Peter. This made a funny story, but I couldn't help imagining a horribly different ending.

Soon after we moved into the new house, Steve made a friend named Jeffery. Joc, like me, had turned against Christian

Science, so I was surprised when she allowed her mother to take Steve and Jeffery to the C.S. Sunday school one morning. The experience didn't seem to affect Steve, but that afternoon when Jeffery cut his finger, he loudly asserted what he'd learned that morning in Sunday School: "There is no blood in God's kingdom!" I dreaded what his parents might say to us, but they never mentioned it.

I took Steve and Julie to the CN Tower. It was exciting to go up the Tower and look down on the city, but what I remember most is having ice cream in the cafeteria afterwards. I asked them what flavours they wanted and left them sitting at a table to keep our place. While I was getting the ice cream, I watched them out of the corner of my eye and saw a man come over and speak to them, but they just kept their heads down. When I joined them at the table, I asked what the man had said. "He asked if he could have the ashtray," Steve said. "What did you say?" I asked. Steve replied, "Nothing. Mom says never talk to strangers." I got such a kick out of this and remembered having heard Joc read a story to them about strange animals one should never talk to.

I also took them to the Toronto Symphony Young People's Concerts for several years. They weren't as interested as I'd hoped, but the reward of a post-concert ice cream cone was a successful motivation. A young prodigy named Jane Coop played at one of these concerts. Years later she made CDs, which I bought and still enjoy.

One winter when Steve was about six, I took him on the train to my brother Bob's farm in Trois Pistoles, Quebec. Bob had a horse and a few other animals. I remember riding the horse bareback, little Steve sitting behind me, his arms around my waist. Every night I read to Steve at bedtime, and Bob would come into the room and watch with great interest. You could see he loved children. (He eventually had four.)

When we got back to Toronto, I started becoming more uncomfortable in the new house. It had a bay window facing the sidewalk, and the dining room was visible from this bay window. When we were eating dinner, sometimes a neighbour would look in. Joc would wave and once even got up and invited her in to sit at the table and chat while we ate dinner. Joc befriended everyone and opened up about everything. I remember one time she was talking about sex with a neighbour, Catherine. As I entered the room, she flashed her daredevil smile at me and told her that she had no complaints about me "in that department." I was mortified!

Catherine had a busy schedule, so Joc offered to make her a cake for a party she was having … as if there was nothing in the world she'd rather do. But when Catherine just left a note and all the ingredients for the cake at our front door without saying anything, Joc was furious!

Joc decided to buy Steve a dog for his seventh birthday. We drove to a house where they had two husky pups, a male and female, the last of the litter. We picked the male because he was so friendly. We paid for him and drove off. I held him on my lap. He kept sighing deeply, his whole body heaving. After five minutes, I said, "Turn around. We'll have to take the other one too." A big mistake! As I later learned, one husky would have been oriented to us. Two huskies relate to each other, excite each other, and run as a pack.

A few months later, I was teaching piano one evening when suddenly there was loud pounding on the front door. It was the woman two doors away. "Your dogs are killing my cat!" she screamed. I raced over to her house. In her driveway was a low sportscar, on top of which was her cat, its fur soaked with the dogs' saliva. The cat was moving hysterically from one side of the roof of the car to the other as the two dogs circled the car, alternately leaping up to try to bite the cat, now from one side, now the other. I pulled the dogs away and reached for the poor cat, who swiped at me and then climbed up the TV tower. I climbed up after it but couldn't reach it. The woman said her cat would come down eventually. I checked next day. The cat had a punctured lung, but the woman wouldn't let me pay the vet's bill.

Another time, Joc and I were walking the dogs on leashes. As we came down the sidewalk, a little kitten saw the dogs and came running down the driveway to play with them. We tried to hold them back, but both dogs attacked the poor kitten, who was seriously hurt—all in an instant!

The neighbours behind had a fence, but if the huskies saw a groundhog in their back yard, in a frenzy they'd hurdle the fence and make short work of the groundhog, leaving it in an ugly little pile inaccessible to us, so we couldn't dispose of the body. The neighbours grew to hate us!

Joc had me build an eight-foot fence around the back yard. One Saturday around dinnertime, in the process of digging, I hit a buried power line and knocked out the electricity for us and a few neighbours. Unable to cook dinner or watch TV, everyone came out to see what had happened. Joc said to Charlie, whose backyard we bordered, "We've got a problem."

He replied, "No, *you've* got a problem."

When my father retired, my parents sold their North York home and bought a little house near Orillia. We visited them with our huskies, who shortly after we arrived made a break and bolted through the forest. We didn't realize there was a farm nearby. Running after them, we arrived to see them trying to attack a calf. Its mother had blood on her and was madly trying to defend the calf, but the huskies kept on attacking from different sides, just as they had with the neighbour's cat. Because they were crazy with bloodlust, it was difficult, but we finally got them leashed.

Dad did a lot of work on his new house. One day while cutting lumber, he sawed the end of his finger almost completely off. Mother was calm as always and drove him to the hospital, where they were able to save his finger.

In 1979, Julie started kindergarten in a French immersion school. The teacher was a young man. On the first day, as each student arrived, he said a loud "Bonjour," and the little girls often burst out crying, but not Julie. Although sensitive, she did not show fear. One little girl entered the room after Julie. When her mother told her to go and talk to one of the girls, she said, "But they're all crying." Her mother pointed at Julie and said, "That girl's not. Go and talk to her."

The school was out of district and Joc had to drive Julie there in the morning and pick her up in the afternoon. One afternoon Joc was so late that a woman who lived across from the school, noticing Julie waiting alone for a very long time, came over and invited her inside until Joc arrived. Again, as with the bathtub incident, this could have had such a bad ending.

Joc liked the teacher, Mr. Weinberg, and started volunteering in his classroom. She spent more and more time with him, told me he was gay, and shared information with him about my sexuality. He came to dinner once and the two of them focused only on each other. I had never seen Joc ignore the children before. For several weeks, Joc and Mr. W. were on the phone frequently, even on weekends. Once when she couldn't reach him, she called Bell and put a tracer on him. He was furious with this invasion of privacy, and the relationship ended at that point.

I began to see Joc as a consumer of people, finding new "friends" and moving more and more into their lives until they could no longer bear her and had to sever the relationship. She liked a teacher in my department and had her husband and her over to dinner two or three times. One of those times, out of the blue, and with no special occasion, she presented them with an expensive gift. They soon ended the relationship.

I realized that this had been the pattern of her relationship with me as well. When we first met, she couldn't get enough of me and frequently came and sat in the CTS auditorium through the long rehearsals for the musicals. I used to wonder; *Doesn't she have things she needs to do?* After a couple of years, she totally lost interest in me. I felt my only functions had been to impregnate her and then make money for the family.

My brother Bob got married in 1980, and six-year-old Julie was the prettiest little flower girl. I was asked to play the organ and practised Mendelssohn's "Wedding March" until I could finally use the foot pedals without sliding onto a wrong note. The wedding took place in London, Ontario in an Anglican church. At the rehearsal, the minister told me not to play the "Wedding March" because it was pagan. I should have objected because my brother's fiancée had requested it, but I played the boring hymns he suggested. I shouldn't have given in, but I was in *his* church, lacked the ego to resist, and didn't want to make a scene and spoil the wedding. I was ashamed afterwards. Audrey and Joe and so many relatives were there, but I got no compliments from anyone, and one man even made negative comments about my music.

CHAPTER 12

Teaching ESL

After I'd been teaching English for eight years, an assistant headship in the department came up. I decided not to apply because the position was Assistant Head of English *in Charge of ESL*. However, my new principal pressured me because the only applicant was a prickly ESL teacher he didn't want to give the job to. I finally yielded, applied, and got the position. ESL students were flooding into Toronto at that time. After just one year as assistant head, I was made head of a new, independent ESL department!

Central Tech's ESL program consisted of three levels of ESL, with the students taking all their classes together for the entire day for three years, after which they entered regular classes in all their subjects, including English. It soon became clear to me that it was inefficient to keep them (except for beginners) totally segregated from the "regular" students from whom they could learn so much English.

I visited a school that had integrated ESL programs, saw how well they worked, and proposed to my principal that CTS ESL students be placed in a regular course as soon as their English was deemed good enough for them to succeed in that course. As a result of being in classes with their English-speaking peers, there was a dramatic improvement in their English!

ESL students were a joy to teach! Most of them respected teachers and really wanted to learn. Many came from countries where teachers were truly valued. The father of one of my students told me, "In Vietnam, a teacher is somewhere above the parents and just below God."

The refugee students had dramatic stories to tell. Two of my Vietnamese students and their father were successful in escaping Vietnam by boat because their father had been a captain in the merchant marine and knew what routes to take to avoid pirates! Another Vietnamese student told me of the pirates' horrible practice of boarding a boat of refugees with hammers to knock out the teeth of anyone who had gold fillings.

One young man told me of escaping Iran and ending up in an American prison because he had forged his documents. When the Iranian hostage crisis happened, a guard refused to give him meals, saying, "No food for you because of the hostages!" This was so ironic because my student *also* disliked the Iranian regime, which was why he had fled the country. I was impressed because he forgave the guard and all those who'd treated him badly.

The most tragic story I heard was from a Cambodian boy, the youngest in his family. His father had been a driver for a leader in the previous government, and when the Khmer Rouge had come for them, the boy had hidden amongst the cows and witnessed the rest of his family being slaughtered. I taught him as a beginner. A few years later I ran into him and he told me about having terrible nightmares and psychological problems because of the memory of this horrendous event.

I had another student from Cambodia whom I'd never seen smile. Then one day he arrived in class beaming. When I asked him what was making him so happy, he replied that he'd received news that his sister and her daughter had escaped from Cambodia to a refugee camp in Thailand. I had read that the chances of an uneducated, unattached female getting out of the refugee camp were slight, so I applied to sponsor them. I made a recording of some classical piano music and sold records, all proceeds going to sponsor these refugees. In a few months the two refugees arrived. I drove out and picked them up and we eventually got them settled. I had to support them for a year. The proceeds from sale of the record didn't go very far, but three generous teachers stepped up to share the costs.

I had expected the worst from my new principal because he had lied to me when he was VP, but so far everything had been fine. However, one day he called me down to his office and told me he'd heard that ESL was all programmed learning, and therefore ESL teachers should have heavier teaching loads than other teachers. Mystified as to why he would say that, I told him that it wasn't true. The following spring, he cut a teacher from my department, even though an increase in ESL student enrolment was projected for the following school year. He had me come to his office to discuss what to do with the teacher's classes in September. When I held up six fingers for each of her six classes and began to describe each class, he roared, "Put those fingers down or I'll break them off!" I was shocked but also ashamed to witness the leader of my school talking like a Mafia thug. (Only years later when I read Comey's description of Trump's methods of intimidation did I realize that my principal had been setting me up for cuts to my department.)

I decided to fight back and ended up giving a speech in front of the director of the Toronto Board, the superintendents, and all the trustees, in which I pointed out the injustice of cutting the teacher when the projected ESL numbers for September were so high. The director called my speech "eloquent," but the OSSTF rep came up to me afterwards, red-faced and furious, and yelled, "How dare you speak in front of the board without letting us know beforehand!"

I "won." The teacher was reinstated, and my principal was transferred to another school, but I was starting to realize that while I had skill in teaching and public speaking, I had little ability in administration, and the socialization and politics of it were unbearably stressful for me.

One day I had to climb several flights of stairs to take something to a Phys Ed. teacher. When I arrived, he pointed out that I was so winded, he was afraid I was going to have a heart attack. I'd never had a weight problem before, but I realized that I had put on about fifty pounds since meeting Jocelyn. She was a superb cook and made very rich, delicious food.

When I told a teacher friend at CTS what the Phys Ed. teacher had said, he invited me to join him at lunchtime to jog on the Central Tech indoor track, where he ran three times a week. I had never played sports or exerted myself in my whole life, so it was really difficult at first, but it gradually got more comfortable. I couldn't believe how good I felt after exercising! When summer school arrived, I began running outside with two other summer-school teachers. Over the next few years, I ran every day, and often long distances. Whenever I got injured from "overuse," I lifted weights instead of running. I lost the fifty pounds, became quite muscular, and in 1981, ran my first marathon. My teacher friend joked, "I've created a monster!"

I started to look for good places to jog to from CTS and found a beautiful ravine park with a paved pathway running through it. There were many bushy areas off the path, and one afternoon an attractive man stopped when he saw me coming toward him. He fixed his gaze on me, walked to the opening leading into a bushy area, stopped again, looked back at me, and headed into the bush. I followed and had gay sex for the first time. It was wonderful! From then on, I jogged to this park regularly, always wondering who I might encounter there. At times it seemed like paradise, although I realized it was dangerous, and I was uncomfortable leading a double life.

I took courses to become an ESL specialist and soon had student teachers. Their professors came to my classroom to see them teach, and I was asked to teach ESL Methodology at the Faculty of Education, U of T (FEUT). I have never worked as hard as I did preparing those lectures.

A CTS art teacher named Alex helped me make a video about ESL teaching and we became friends, eventually discovering that we were both gay. For years we enjoyed getting together to see a film and then going out to dinner afterwards.

I started a Master's in Teaching English at U of T. It consisted of eight courses. However, after completing the first two courses and doing very well, my FEUT timetable was increased so much I had to let the MA go.

After I had taught at FEUT for a few years, another instructor told me that I should apply to direct ESL courses at York University, which I did and got the job. The pay was phenomenal—a six-month-a-year, one-night-a-week part-time job that added 50 per cent of what I made in my full-time job! With just a BA, I got to hire lecturers with PhDs, hear them lecture, and try out their suggested approaches in my classroom.

However, after a few years I lost the job of director because the York University Professors Union stopped allowing people without graduate degrees to direct courses. My lucrative job was gone just like that.

One day when I was at the faculty, I saw my high school geography teacher, Mr. Baine, walking down the hall toward me. I'd heard that he'd left Downsview Collegiate to teach there. It had been over twenty years, but when he saw me, he said "Grant … Reynolds!" I told him I was surprised he remembered my name, and he said, "How could I forget someone your age who could play Franck's *Symphonic Variations?*" What a wonderful compliment! Once again, my music helped bolster my fragile ego.

While I was teaching, courses called Ontario Academic Credits (OACs) were developed for students planning to go to university. ESL students tended to do extremely well in all their OACs except for English. To expect them to measure up to the level of students who had grown up speaking English and taken English courses for twelve years was unreasonable, so an English for ESL Students OAC course was developed, and in my school I taught it. We studied the same literature as the regular OAC English course, except for Shakespeare.

I taught this course every semester until I retired, and it was the high point of my teaching career. When I had switched from English to ESL teaching, I had been reluctant to give up my Grade 13 English course, but my ESL English OAC students were much higher achievers, got more scholarships, and valued their education more.

For a professional development day, a professor from U of T came to talk to the CTS staff about teaching reading. After the talk, I went up and thanked him and invited him to come and see my OAC English class. I had learned a lot about teaching reading from the lecturers I'd hired for the York U courses. When the professor came to see my class, he was amazed because I had incorporated all the reading techniques he advocated. A couple of years later, the Faculty of Education needed someone to teach reading, and this professor suggested me. The head of reading asked him about my qualifications, but the prof said "It doesn't matter. He would be good." I had no official qualifications, but I ended up teaching reading.

Around this time, I started giving an annual spring recital at CTS. Shortly after the first one, I saw a former student in the hall. I hadn't seen him for ten years, but he was very special and I immediately remembered his name, just as Mr. Baine had remembered mine after many years. After graduating, John had started studying piano and was now playing at an advanced level—a very unusual feat. He joined me in future recitals, and we soon became good friends.

In 1990, Nelson Mandela came to Central Tech. I learned "*Nkosi Sikeleli- Africa*" on the piano and helped teach it to the choir, but then I found out it was sung a cappella, so I sang in the choir. Mandela had a presence I'd never experienced before. Hearing him inspired me deeply.

After a few years, my new principal said that ESL had grown so much I would get an assistant head. Not too long before that, I had attended an ESL reception. One of the speakers was an ESL student who had been coached by a teacher named Barbara. When the student was about to speak, she looked over at Barb nervously, and Barb flashed her a beautiful smile, which seemed to calm the student and give her confidence. I thought, *That's the kind of teacher I'd like to have as my assistant head.* I invited Barb to apply, and she was successful in getting the position. We eventually became close friends. She was an excellent pianist and took part in our annual recitals.

When I started at Central Tech, it was believed that the school was too tough to have a woman as principal. However, times were changing, and eventually we got our first female principal. The male principals had kept a distance, but Verna talked to me like an equal and even came into the ESL office to find out how everyone was doing from time to time.

In the 1990s, there was a lot of deliberate disruption in education caused by Mike Harris's Conservative government. We went on strike. I was picketing with a group of teachers one day when a reporter came up and asked me about the strike. I spoke at length about what was wrong with the Harris government. Then he asked me what I would do if the strike continued for a long time. "I'd have to sell my house," I replied.

I was thrilled because that evening I was going to be on the CBC national news! Even my relatives in Winnipeg were watching! However, when the piece about the strike arrived, my articulate explanation of what was wrong with the government was left out entirely, and the interview consisted only of the part about selling my house! After that, whenever reporters wanted to interview a CTS teacher, my principal referred them to me, and once she asked Barb as well.

I started to be more out in the open. I walked with CTS students in the AIDS walk, no longer worried that people might think I was gay. In 1998, I was MC for the Black History Month assembly. I invited a former student, Hamlin Grange, to speak. As a successful Black newscaster, he was a great role model. I showed the video of his coverage of Nelson Mandela's visit in 1990 for CBC TV news.

Also in 1998, a popular CTS student named Duane Robotham was stabbed to death. There was talk among his friends about avenging his death. His mother came to the school to speak, and

I was asked to play before and after she spoke. The auditorium was packed. She began by saying, "If you had told me one of my children would be knifed to death, I would have expected it to be one of my other children, not Duane." She talked about his fine qualities and the futility of getting revenge for his death by doing more killing. Her speech was compelling, and the students were very moved, as was I. After she finished speaking, I began playing again, and when I finished, I turned to see this generous woman standing behind me, waiting to thank me for the music.

Around the time of the *fatwa* on Salman Rushdie, the Toronto Board Librarians held a weekend retreat on Islam, which I attended. There were four Islamic speakers: a professor, an Imam, and two graduate students. All the speakers, except the professor, argued that Rushdie had insulted the Prophet and *obviously* must die. I remember one of them saying, "What would you do if *your Jesus* was insulted?" I heard one of the teachers quietly mention "*Life of Brian*," but audience participation was not invited. The chasm between us liberal teachers and the authoritarian Islamic speakers was as wide as could be. In what was obviously an unintended consequence, I came away from the retreat horrified at how brutal Islam seemed.

I decided to take piano lessons again, so I called William Aide, but he had more students than he could manage. He recommended a former student of his, Richard. I went to hear Richard play "Rhapsody in Blue" with the Mississauga Symphony. He was brilliant. I took lessons from him for twelve years.

I had continued running and lifting weights for many years and had always changed and showered in the Phys Ed office, but one day I was told to move to the pool change room in the basement. I will never forget that Friday. I was in the shower room at the end of the school day. The swim coach was leaving and yelled, "Grant, are you OK?" I didn't know what he meant, so I said yes. When I finished showering, I went to go into the change room, but the door was locked. To my horror, I realized that my clothes and, more importantly, *my keys* were there! I would be locked in this small shower room for the whole weekend until Monday when classes resumed!

I went into a panic, and like a trapped animal frantically went around and around the room looking for a place to escape. After a few minutes, I forced myself to calm down and think of a solution. I looked around and noticed a metal grid near the bottom of the solid wooden door that led to the gym. With my fists I hammered at it for a long time and was able to eventually dislodge it and crawl through the small opening that led to the gym. With just a towel on, I ran through the gym and into the hall, which was deserted except for one girl. When I called for help, she looked briefly at me, this man with just a towel around his waist, then hightailed it down the hall!

Finally, I found a caretaker, who let me into the change room where my clothes and keys were.

CHAPTER 13

Family Life

After Julie was born, our only socializing took place with Joc's family. Her sister had two children about the same age as ours. They lived in the Beaches, so we were often there and frequently went for walks along the boardwalk. I had known Joc's sister and her husband in the Forum and got along well with both of them, especially my brother-in-law. He was British but had grown up in Argentina, where his father had been a diplomat. Joc's father often called him "twinkle toes" behind his back, and I was struck by the irony of my father-in-law implying that he was gay and assuming I was straight.

We often went to Halton Hills to walk our dogs and then have a picnic with Joc's parents, her sisters, and their families. I eventually came to enjoy these outings. It felt good to be expressing emotions, relaxing, laughing, and joking.

Joc's father sold yachts. Once he took us out on Lake Ontario in a big sailboat called the *Bernice*. He was skipper and my mother-in-law was steering when suddenly a group of racing boats rounded an island and came straight toward us. He instructed her to tack in a certain direction, but she panicked and did the opposite. We almost hit one of the boats, which went by us with everyone on board yelling curses at us.

Sometimes we would go camping at Killbear Park. By this time, Joc's father and I were very friendly. Once he recited an entire poem for me while we were driving around the campground.

He was a quick wit. I remember when we saw a family of racoons, and Joc's mother asked, "Why are some of them so small?" Without missing a beat, he replied, "They're babies. That's just nature's way."

Joc's father invited me over to watch the Grey Cup one year. I had thought I hated football, but I had a great time watching the game with him and my brother-in-law.

Joc's father was crazy about his dog, Jill, who was inclined to be vicious. I was walking in a park with him one day. Jill was off the leash, and when a jogger came running toward us, Jill ran right up to him barking furiously, as if to attack. The jogger, visibly shaken, said, "Mister, your dog should be on a leash!"

He replied, "Well, you shouldn't be jogging!" With a look of disbelief, the jogger ran off.

My mother-in-law worried about Steve because I hadn't taught him how to play sports. She went to the Olympium and asked about programs for little boys who weren't developing normally. Steve was placed in a swimming course, and only when Joc took him to the first class did she realize that it was a course for children with *various challenges*.

In the class he made a friend named Jason, whose mother asked Joc to bring Steve over to her house so the boys could play. Over coffee it became clear to Joc that Jason's mother was becoming increasingly curious about just what Steve's challenges were. She would mention problems her son had and then pause, waiting for similar disclosures from Joc, but Joc was not forthcoming. By the time they had their second get-together, Jason's mother was clearly desperate to find out. After several unsuccessful attempts to get answers from Joc, she abandoned subtlety and suddenly blurted out, "What *is* Stephen's problem?" Joc, feeling it was time to put Jason's mother out of her misery, told the story of how Steve had accidentally ended up in the class.

Picking up on her mother's worry about Steve's lack of paternal athletic guidance, Joc decided to go one step further and enrolled both Steve and me in a Tae Kwan Do program. When she told me, I was not pleased, but I forced myself to go for Steve's sake. Right from the beginning, Steve excelled in Tae Kwan Do. After a few weeks he was able to win matches against much older boys. He liked it so much that in a short time I started to look forward to our outings together.

The two instructors, brothers from Korea, were very strict. I thought I was supposed to be macho and show no fear. When one of them used me to demonstrate to the class how to get an opponent to yield by bending his thumb back, I looked the teacher directly in the eye and showed no reaction to the excruciating pain, but instead of admiring my bravery, the teacher looked more and more furious and increased the pressure to the point where I thought my thumb would break right off and I'd never play the piano again. Only then did I realize that I was supposed to yield to make the teacher look good, which I quickly did.

A few months later, Julie joined the class. She was the youngest in the group. The instructors always tried to look tough, and if anyone spoke out, they punished the whole class by making us all do push ups. Once during one of these class punishments, when Julie was unsuccessfully trying to do push ups, both of her barrettes fell out onto the floor. That was the only time the instructors ever smiled. They just couldn't help it.

Soon we were to go to tournaments, which cost money, so Joc decided to end Tae Kwon Do. Steve was very disappointed and so was I because it was so good for Steve! Joc had forced me into it, but I'd persevered and now she was forcing us out of it. She had to control and often said, "I'm always right," with her jaw set, daring anyone to disagree.

Steve never forgot Tae Kwan Do, and when he started high school, he joined the wrestling team. In Grade 9 he lost every match, but his coach kept telling him, "If you keep on trying, by the time you're in Grade 13, you'll be the Etobicoke champion." Steve did keep on trying and, sure enough, by Grade 13 he was the champion in his weight class in all of Etobicoke.

For a long period of time, I had little contact with my parents. They had bought a winter place in Texas, so when Julie was about twelve, we flew there to visit them. I gave a short piano recital there. My father was president of Pine to Palm Park, a mobile home park, and we went to hear him give a speech, which was excellent. He enjoyed himself there. After Mother died, I saw a photo of him in the park. He and two other men were in drag riding bicycles, and Dad had a big smile on his face. Not the Dad I knew!

Joc had been unhappy almost as soon as we moved into our second house, so right away I said we should sell it, but she was dead set against it. We lived in that house for seven long years.

Our third house was a semi-detached in Etobicoke. Just after we moved, the public high school across the street became a Catholic high school, so Steve had to go out of district to Silverthorn Collegiate for high school. It turned out to be a blessing because Silverthorn was in a better area and was the

Etobicoke Board of Education's flagship school. Steve, whose main report card comment in elementary school had been "must pay attention," started to flourish. First, he won the top mark for his school in a province-wide math test. His math teacher called Joc, suspicious about how Steve could have done so well considering his mediocre performance in elementary school. At the end of the year, we got invited to commencement to watch Steve get an award for having one of the highest averages in Grade 9. When I asked him about his success in high school, he said that in elementary school he could never figure out what the teachers wanted, but in high school he learned right away that if you studied hard for tests and exams, you'd get high marks. Not only did he continue to get high marks for the rest of high school, but in Grade 12 he became student council president and was honoured for his exceptional leadership skills and presented with a citizenship award by Judge Piccinini.

Julie got her driver's license as soon as she turned sixteen, and a motorcycle soon after that. I tied myself in knots worrying about her safety, but she never had an accident.

Both Steve and Julie went to many leadership and anti-racist camps and developed so wonderfully! I remember walking with Steve one day when he was in high school. A younger teenage boy who was coming toward us muttered "faggot" as we passed. Steve's maturity impressed me. He didn't get angry; he just wondered what was troubling the boy.

Julie went to hear Gloria Steinem speak, and when she told an older girl how inspiring Steinem was, the girl said she had reservations about Steinem because she'd heard she was a lesbian. Julie just stared at her without saying anything, and the girl got very uncomfortable. Later on in university, Julie would dance with the gay boys just to bug the other girls, who would whisper to each other, "Doesn't she know he's gay?"

Most of Steve's high school friends weren't white. I thought it wonderful that skin colour didn't seem to be an issue. Sanjay, the boy Steve most often hung around with, had brown skin. One Friday evening there was a knock on the front door. I opened it to see Sanjay dressed up as a cowboy to go with Steve to a dance at their school. He had a string tie on, and his collar was crooked. I said, "There's something wrong with your collar."

Looking very upset, Sanjay asked, "What's wrong with my *colour*?" Explaining what I meant, I reached over and straightened his collar, but I almost broke down because I saw how big an issue skin colour still was in the pain so clearly written on Sanjay's face!

Despite what she'd said when we first met, Joc's parents, especially her father, were everything to her. Sometimes she had them over for breakfast on weekends. One Sunday morning when it was well past the time they were to arrive, she was wondering what was wrong. She called, and her brother, who always slept really late, answered the phone. When she asked what he was doing up so early, he told her he had just walked the dog. Her father was the one who always walked the dog, though, and when she said flippantly, "Dad must be in pretty bad shape," her brother replied, "That's not funny, Joc. *Dad died last night.*" I choke up after all these years when I think of that morning. It was so cruel to tell Joc that way. It hurt her so deeply.

In July 1988, we went to Napanee for my dad's seventy-third birthday. A week later I got a call from my brother who, sobbing, told me that Dad had died the previous night and to get there as fast as I could. I wanted to leave Toronto right away, but we had only one car, and Joc really took her time. (She hated Dad, often calling him "Dick the prick," even in front of the children.)

When we finally arrived, Mother asked me to call a list of people to inform them Dad had died. It was difficult, but I called and delivered the news successfully, with one exception. I called a cousin of Dad and said that it was Grant. When I told her that Dad had died, she screamed and then, weeping, asked me about the details. When I gave them, she realized that I was a different Grant. She had thought I was her nephew, Grant, calling to say her brother had died!

Mother got a man from the Kingston Christian Science Church to do a memorial service. At the reception, Joc noticed Mother's balcony railing was in disrepair and insisted Steve and I rebuild it for her. Mother didn't want it done, and we didn't want to do it, but Joc made us. A new foundation had to be put in, and it took us several days to complete the new deck.

Mother sold her house and bought one close to Bob. When the cold weather came, she got sick and after a few days was barely able to get out of bed. She tried to pretend she was fine, and for many days refused to let Bob take her to the hospital. Finally Bob called me. He was desperate, and asked me to talk to her, because I understood C.S. However, I didn't bring up C.S. I simply said, "You always taught us to be reasonable. You're not doing well and Bob is very upset. Please let him take you to the hospital." To everyone's relief she agreed to go. It turned out she had double pneumonia because she'd waited so long, but she recovered, although it permanently weakened her heart.

After Dad died, Mother never seemed happy, which surprised me. I thought she'd feel free of what I saw as his oppressive nature. I remembered visiting my brother Barrie years before. He told Joc and me how happy Mother and Dad were together. Joc said, "Yes, but they shouldn't have had children."

I suggested to Mother that we talk on the phone once a week.

She called me dutifully every Sunday at a set time but was obviously uncomfortable. At the end of our stilted conversations, she'd say, "Well, I think that's about all," and we'd say goodbye. I wished I'd never suggested the weekly calls because they really got me down.

When Steve was in Grade 13, he told us he wanted to go to Queen's and take commerce because it was the hardest course to get into. I pointed out that that wasn't a good reason and that he'd never been particularly interested in finance.

Shortly after that, we had Brian and his wife, Lesley, to dinner. I had first encountered Brian when he was a student in my teachers' course. After that I sometimes hired him as a supply teacher. He told me he wanted a permanent position but would wait until one came up in my department. When it did, he applied and got the job. He was one of the most caring teachers I ever saw. I remember a student of his telling me that Brian was just like a father to everyone in his class.

Always well-meaning, before dinner Brian told Joc that I was under a lot of stress with my many teaching jobs and suggested she get a job to help relieve the pressure on me. Then during dinner, he asked Steve about his educational plans, and he and Lesley said they thought going away to university was a great idea! Joc, who wanted Steve to go to university in Toronto, and resented Brian's suggestion that she get a job, was not pleased. There was tension in the air for the rest of the evening.

Steve did get into commerce at Queen's and into residence. Before he left, he offered me his room, since it was obvious that Joc and I were having a lot of trouble getting along. I was sad to see him go. After a few weeks, Joc told me he was homesick. It was very uncomfortable for me coming from a family in which no affection was ever shared, but I steeled myself, called

Steve, and ended the call by telling him I loved him. He replied brusquely, "I love you too." I called again in a week and again ended the call with "I love you." Steve replied, "You don't have to say it every time." But of course I did, because if I didn't keep saying it, I'd never say it again.

After Christmas, Steve told me he hated commerce and had switched to general arts. I said, "Good. The main thing is that you study something you enjoy."

"You mean you're not angry?" he asked. When I said no, he seemed as relieved as he had when he was six and I had assured him that doing a bad thing did not make him a bad person.

CHAPTER 14

Someday He'll Come Along

After Joc's father died, her mother sold the house in Toronto and moved to a cottage near Thunder Bay, where she'd grown up. Joc and the kids went there every summer.

In the summer of 1991, when they were away, I met a young man in High Park. I was too nervous to *really* look at him during our encounter, but he seemed nice. His name was Carl, and we agreed to meet again in the same place the following Saturday. When the day arrived, I got there early and sat on a picnic table at the top of the hill at the south end of the park, wondering if he'd show up. After a few minutes, I saw a handsome man climbing the hill. He smiled at me, and it was like the sun coming up over the horizon! This time we talked a lot. He told me he supervised the boys in a Korean International School and was off only on weekends. He was from Prince Edward Island and was only twenty-four years old.

The third time we met was at Sunnyside. The breeze from Lake Ontario made it a little chilly, so I lent Carl my sweater, which gave me a special feeling of connection to him. I think that by the third meeting, you get a sense of what a relationship is going to be like. Carl seemed as excited by me as I was by him. There was so much chemistry between us. I felt comfortable talking to him, and I loved looking into his handsome face. After we parted and I was driving home, I heard "The Man I Love" on my radio, sung by the San Francisco Gay Men's Chorus. Hearing men singing the words sent shivers up and down my spine. I thought, *So this is what it's like to fall in love!*

Soon after that, Joc and the kids arrived home. A couple of days later, a friend called to thank me for taking him out to dinner for his birthday. Joc picked up the extension and over-heard him talking. After I hung up, she went ballistic! She told me to get out, as she had many times, but this time I felt I could do it. Carl gave me something to look forward to. Also, I had bought a keyboard in case I had to leave. My take-home pay was $2,900 a month, so I decided to give Joc $2,000 for Julie and her and keep $900 for myself. I forgot to factor in that they lived in a house I was paying for. I could barely live on $900 a month. I had to look for a low-rent place. It took me a couple of months, but eventually I found a basement apartment in a house owned by a nice young couple.

On moving day, I had movers take my pull-out couch, my keyboard, and some other heavy things, and I took a few loads in my car. In the evening when I was about to leave with the last load, Joc proposed watching a video, but I said I had to go. I felt bad because she'd also kicked out her sister, who had been living with us, and both of us were leaving on the same day. I headed to the highway but started to wonder if I should go back and watch a movie with Joc. I slowed down but then realized there was no turning back this time. I had to go through with it, no matter how difficult. And it was difficult. Here I was at forty-seven about to begin living alone for the first time in my life. What a pathetic creature I was! I'd gone right from Mother to Joc and had never even made a meal before.

After a month or so, I arranged to go to the bank with Joc to set up an account into which her monthly support payments would be deposited.

The woman setting up the account for us said, "Excuse me, I know I shouldn't ask, but are you the couple who are splitting up? You seem to get along so well."

Carl stayed over most weekends and it was wonderful.

I had always intended to wait until both my children were away at university before leaving Joc, and felt very bad leaving Julie, who was in Grade 12 and still had two years of high school left. Once she called me very distressed about the way Joc was treating her, and I drove to meet her and try to provide some comfort.

Later on, she came to visit me in my new apartment. I'd forgotten I had a photo of Carl sitting on my bookshelf, and she asked who the handsome man was. When I told her I was gay, a tear ran down her cheek, but she seemed to accept who I was. I was more worried about how Steve would react, being a boy. When he came home for Christmas, I took him out to dinner and came out to him. He seemed completely fine with it, to my immense relief.

The basement apartment was clean and looked nice during the day, but I had trouble sleeping there because there was a furnace between me and the only exit, and the windows were too small for me to escape through if there was a fire. I didn't have enough money to get a better place but came across a book on how you could make money through owning an income home. I suggested to Carl that we go in together on one.

Every weekend our agent took us to look at income homes.

He showed us one I thought was perfect—a proper triplex with three nice, spacious apartments—but Carl didn't like it. Then we looked at a single-family dwelling made into three apartments, which he liked, so we made an offer on it, which was accepted. I had quite a struggle getting a mortgage. At the bank we found out we couldn't count Carl's income because he'd been in his job less than six months. We had bought the house jointly, but when I realized that owning only half of the house meant I could only claim 50 per cent of the expenses against my income, I got Carl to sign over the entire house to me.

The day we moved in, Carl, always a joker, tried to carry me over the threshold and hurt his back. He had to quit his job at the school. I needed his income, but after he recovered, he wanted to go to university, not find another job. I started to realize he was the male version of Joc. Why work when you could live off someone else? However, we did have good times together. We both loved films and saw quite a few together. My friends liked him. We would get together with my friend, Barb, and two teachers in my department and their wives, Hannes and Joanna, and Brian and Lesley, who were totally accepting. Steve and Julie liked Carl too. I remember them and their friends laughing their heads off at his jokes and kidding.

The income home turned out to be a nightmare! I needed the rent money to pay the huge mortgage every month, but even though the basement apartment was usually rented, the high-yielding upstairs apartment was often vacant. Because they were adaptations from a single-family home, none of the apartments were adequate, and something was always going wrong. I had to race around getting broken appliances repaired or replaced. One rainy morning the upstairs tenant came down in her robe. She'd been in the shower when a paint bubble on the ceiling broke and water came flooding down. Later I found out that the roof had blown off!

When Carl's mother came to visit, we set up separate bedrooms. They slept in "Carl's bedroom," and I was in the other room. (She was obviously suspicious, though.) She had a strong Newfoundland accent, and most of the time I couldn't understand a word she was saying. I could only say "Pardon me?" so many times before I had to pretend I understood her. She only stayed a few days, but then his brother came and stayed for a long time. He too had a strong accent, and his words were truncated and died in his throat. Carl spoke perfectly and told me he'd learned standard English by watching TV. Eventually his brother found a girlfriend and moved out.

Carl got into drama at York U and spent more and more time there. When I tried to have one dinner a week together, he'd say he had to go to York to study. He'd also go to get marijuana and stay out for long periods of time. With all the work of the income home added to my teaching, I had no time for anything else. Carl started smoking, which irritated me. We drifted farther and farther apart. Early in 1995, he told me he was leaving. We'd been together for over three years. I was devastated but got support from my friends. When I told Barb we were breaking up, tears came into her eyes, and Hannes called to say he was sorry to hear about the breakup.

It was an extended breakup. Carl would come back to the apartment when I was away but be gone by the time I got home. Eventually I found out that he was in a relationship with a man who'd come to lecture in his drama course. Carl had an answering machine that played his messages out loud, and it was painful to hear this man's messages to him.

By this time Julie was at Lakehead University in Thunder Bay, and I went to visit her on the March Break. On the long bus trip there, I was sad and wrote a song about the breakup, but as soon as I saw Julie I felt better.

When I returned to Toronto, I was still depressed about Carl leaving, but I came across a card he'd left advertising the underwear party at the Barn. Carl had mentioned it, but I never had the nerve to go. Now I needed to get out and meet someone, so I steeled myself and headed there. I arrived to see dozens of men clad only in their underwear! Upstairs there was a maze, which I entered. I saw an attractive man who seemed to be trying to get away from another man, so I approached him. His name was Andy. We got a taxi back to my place and spent the night together. In the morning we had breakfast on my deck and talked for a couple of hours before I walked him to the subway. Like me, the previous night had been the first time he'd ever gone to an underwear party. Andy was twenty-nine. He worked with physically and intellectually challenged people and had a very successful career. He often had to work on weekends, but we got together when we could. He loved dancing, and I went with him to dances, although I wasn't a good dancer. He kidded me about my dancing once, saying, "That's not dancing ... that's jogging."

Andy came to my house a few times, but I was only at his place once, when the owner (who also lived there) was away for the weekend. It was gorgeous and had a beautiful white grand piano in the living room. I asked Andy if I could play it, and afterwards I sat down on the sofa and looked up at the beautiful, two-storey-high ceiling. Glancing down, I had a surreal experience I will never forget. There on the coffee table was a copy of *Toronto Life* with the very room I was sitting in on the front cover! I looked up the article and photos of other parts of the house and read about its history.

In a short time I fell in love with Andy. This relationship was different from my relationship with Carl. I had the deepest respect for Andy, and I grew to totally trust him.

My brothers and I had arranged an eightieth birthday party for my mother in September 1995 at the Valhalla Inn in Etobicoke. Many people, mostly relatives, came, including all ten of her nephews and nieces, several of them from the United States. On the Friday evening we had a reception, and on Saturday evening we had a dinner. That night I stayed at the hotel, and when I went to my room, I felt sorry for myself because I hadn't seen Andy for a couple of weeks. That night he was finally available, but I was busy.

During the following week I saw an attractive man when I was jogging, and I cheated on Andy. As a result of the encounter, I got crabs. Andy and I were to get together in a few days, and I should have told him I was sick and couldn't meet him, but I was so upset I couldn't think clearly. I met up with him, and when I told him I'd cheated on him, he was deeply hurt and ended the relationship. He had warned me he would not tolerate any cheating. He had a reputation for having high standards. Once, for his birthday, his friends had paid for a hustler and placed bets as to whether Andy would have sex with him. He wouldn't, even though the gorgeous man was paid for.

I called Andy repeatedly and begged for another chance, and I remember taking a gift for his birthday and hanging it on his door. All to no avail. He would "forgive, but not forget." But I could never forgive myself for my stupidity and lack of discipline. I became depressed, but circumstances were very different from the time I'd tried to kill myself. Suicide never occurred to me. I now had children who loved me and supported me, and I would never do anything to hurt them.

Steve came over to see how I was doing, and when he saw how down I was, he got quite angry, insisting I had to pull myself together and stop moping around! I'd been impressed that Andy had volunteered with the AIDS Committee, so I decided that's what I would do. Steve offered to come with me to the first meeting, where we got an introduction to what the AIDS Committee does, and I had to choose what to volunteer for. I chose going to bathhouses to talk about safe sex, and it helped me to stop focusing on myself and get back on my feet.

I also looked up Dr. Lamon and called him. He was willing to be my psychiatrist again. Twenty years before when I had last seen him, his practice was near Dundas and Yonge. Now he saw patients in the coach house behind his home in Rosedale.

The second place I went to for help was SLAA (Sex and Love Addicts Anonymous), a twelve-step program. I attended every week for three or four years. We were mostly gay men and a few women, and we talked about our addictive behaviour and how much harm it had done to our lives. Participants were sincere, but some were pretty extreme, like the man who counted the number of months he'd gone without masturbating. I bought and read all the books I could about sex addiction, put covers on them to hide the titles, and read them voraciously. Once I was reading one of them on a crowded bus, always trying to shield the print from the view of other passengers, when the woman sitting beside me said, "Oh, that really looks interesting!"

I didn't know how to respond, but I forced myself to smile, and replied, "Umm … yes, it is."

When a weekend retreat at a monastery in Guelph was announced, I decided to go. I thought others in my group would also attend, but I was the only one. I arrived at the monastery to find that many of the participants were men from a nearby detention centre, some of whom had committed sex crimes. They seemed to all be straight, so I was a little hesitant to tell my story, but I forced myself to. Afterwards, a tough-looking man came over and thanked me, saying he'd never before realized the struggles a gay man had to go through.

When the retreat was over, I got a ride back to Toronto. The driver, who turned out to be a psychiatrist, spoke about Marianne Williams and her book, *A Return to Love.* The next day I bought it and was fascinated that she wrote that the opposite of love was *fear.* I realized I was terrified of people but could actually calm myself down by replacing my fear with love. Her book was based on *A Course in Miracles,* which I also bought. I liked it because it was not dogmatic.

In another attempt to overcome my depression, I joined a drama class at Metropolitan Community Church, Toronto (MCCT). It was a lot of fun and I met many friendly people, including a man named Jeff, who became a close friend. I joined many other groups at MCCT, such as Men's Coming Out and Relationship Rebuilding, where we had to do a project with a partner. Mine was to go with one of the women in the course and take salsa lessons at El Convento Rico. We had so much fun!

I didn't believe in God, but the people in the courses at MCCT were so friendly I eventually decided to try a church service. MCCT had a mostly gay congregation. The people welcomed me, the music was great, and the minister, Brent Hawkes, gave sermons that were excellent and focused on relationships, not religious dogma. I remember the day I joined the church. Seeing how troubled I looked, Brent Hawkes asked me what was wrong, but I didn't tell him about my atheism.

I also joined an addiction group at MCCT, which included all addictions, such as alcohol and drugs, as well as sex. The text we used explained addiction as a search for something to replace God, but it claimed that only God could truly satisfy us. The group had two leaders, a woman and a man. The woman was an ex-Christian Scientist, so the two of us kidded a lot about it. The man had been sexually abused when he was young, and during the course, the story broke about the Maple Leaf Gardens coach abusing boys. He told us he had been one of those boys. Seeing the news had caused him to relive the horrors of his abuse, and, in front of us, he broke down completely and wept.

One Sunday I played a Chopin "Prelude" during the service. A woman came up to me afterwards, complimented me on my playing, and asked if I would be her teacher. Her name was Marilyn, and she became another close friend.

MCCT was an exciting place to be. Sometimes famous people dropped in to attend a service. I met Jack Layton, Louise Pitre, and others. I got to attend one of the first gay weddings in the world. There were reporters in the church from as far away as Japan.

CHAPTER 15

Men

MCCT was a great way to meet men. I was becoming much more outgoing. I joined the choir, and when a woman in the choir invited me to her holy union, I forced myself to go over to a handsome man I had noticed in the social hall, introduce myself, and ask him if he'd go with me. He looked quite taken aback, questioned me a lot, and finally, almost reluctantly, agreed to go. His name was Parker and he lived in Hamilton.

On the day of the holy union, I met him at the Greyhound bus station. We went back to my place, and he seemed very wary that I might make a move on him, so I was scrupulous in giving him total privacy as he changed for the event. The holy union was on a cruise boat in the Toronto Harbour. When we boarded in the late afternoon, I wondered where the two brides were, but I soon heard someone shout, "There they are!" I looked out on Lake Ontario to see them approaching in a motorboat as the guests cheered. After the wedding and meal, the dancing started. It was a slightly chilly evening, and Parker and I danced every slow dance. It was so romantic and exciting!

At midnight we disembarked and got a cab back to my place.

When we got into my house, I was very circumspect. I showed Parker the separate room and bed he would sleep in and said good night. After a few minutes, he came over to my door and asked if I'd like to cuddle. I was surprised because he'd been so wary of me up to this point. I approached him very hesitantly, but soon we were making love, and it was great!

The next morning, though, he seemed distant, almost hostile. In the cab on the way to the bus station when we passed "Little Italy" signs, he said, "Your area should be called *Little Sodom and Gomorrah.*"

I called Parker a couple of times about getting together again, but he wasn't interested. However, just before Pride, he called me to ask if he could stay at my place. I said, "No, I'm not willing to just be a convenient place for you to stay."

I was still pursuing men in search of a replacement for Andy, but I had to learn that men operated very differently from me. Most had egos and directly communicated what they wanted. I had joined a social group for gays and lesbians called "Out and Out." In the summers they had an event called "Jamboree" at a camp in Haliburton. There was every imaginable activity, from acting sessions to massage classes to sports. When a handsome man named Gavin and I were partners in a massage class, he seemed excited like me but said people would gossip like crazy if we connected.

The next summer, Out and Out went to Toronto Island for a picnic and games, and I saw Gavin there. After we got back to the city, he approached me on Church Street, said that he found me hot, and asked if I'd like to have sex. He told me he wasn't interested in a relationship with me. He really liked this other man I'd seen him with at the island. We spent a great night together. The next time I saw him he was living with this other man. I was starting to learn to have no regrets, to just accept a wonderful gift like this and let it go.

The men I knew weren't always business-like. Some were very romantic. Once I was at a musical party on a warm summer evening. Most people were outside, and I stayed out with them socializing for as long as I could. However, I can only make small talk for so long, and finally I went inside, sat down at the piano, and played a Chopin waltz. The windows were open, and when I finished, everyone outside clapped loudly. Ronald, a young man from MCCT who had just finished his BA and was going away to law school in the fall, asked me if I'd accompany him. He sang some songs from a musical so well that I wondered if he'd had a lead part in a high school or university production. He stood behind me as he sang. There was a mirror above the piano, and from time to time I'd look at him and notice how attractive he was, especially when he was singing. I felt so good because he appreciated my musical accompaniment. We connected through music.

When the party was coming to an end, Ronald asked me if I'd like to go for a drink. I thought he was just being friendly. We went to a bar on Church Street and had a beer, after which he looked at me directly and asked, *"What would you like to happen now?"* I'll never forget those words! I hadn't seen this coming. It was one of the most romantic moments of my whole life! It took a while for me to still my beating heart. I gulped, steeled myself, and said I'd like us to go back to my place. We had a great night together, but I knew it was another gift I had to just be grateful for and let go.

Some men are terrified of commitment. At MCCT I met Pete. He was a little younger than me and had a high position in the civil service. We dated, and he seemed to really like me. He even gave me an expensive leather jacket. He lived out of town but came into Toronto on Sundays. After church, we would have lunch at a restaurant on Church Street and walk around the gay village. I'd say hello to people I knew as we passed, and once I remember Pete exclaiming, "Is there anybody on Church Street you don't know?" This made me realize how out-going I was becoming. Pete and I were together for only a few months, because when I jokingly mentioned something about living together, he visibly tightened up and that was the end of our relationship.

After the breakup, other friends from church got me to help Pete move. He had bought a condo in Toronto. I was partnered up with a friend of Pete's named Dave. We loaded Dave's car with small items and drove them to Pete's new place, making a couple of trips. Dave was charming and very attractive, but he was married. I'd sold my house, and a short time after I'd helped Pete move, I got a call from him wondering if he and Dave could come over to see the apartment I'd moved into. It was obvious they had been drinking. They didn't stay long.

A couple of days later, I got a call from Dave. He said he'd lost his sunglasses and wanted to come over and see if he'd left them at my place.

I thought it highly unlikely, but Dave was so attractive, I was only too happy to play along. Sure enough, there were no missing sunglasses, and that day was the beginning of our relationship. I really liked him, and we seemed very compatible. He was a social worker and, like me, was serious about his career. And what par-allels! He was ten years younger than me and had a son ten years younger than Steve and a daughter ten years younger than Julie. He lived in Mississauga but worked in Toronto and would come to my place while downtown. One time he couldn't park at the gas station across the street from me, so I went out to let him into the underground parking. When he got home, his wife said a "friend" had called her to say he had seen Dave in the gay village with another man. Dave told his wife he was just meeting with a client in the village. I really empathized with Dave because his situation was so similar to what mine had been, and, like me, he obviously loved his children. I didn't want him to lose them. He only visited about once a week, but I treasured the time we had together. I would gladly have spent the rest of my life with him. After a few months we broke up, though. I cared deeply about him, but it was just too dangerous for him.

For a while I dated a nurse named Romeo. He worked at a hospital on the same street my second-floor apartment faced. One day I looked out my window and saw him walking to work. I ran out onto my balcony yelling "Romeo! Romeo!" before I realized that I was acting out a scene from Shakespeare!

I dated many men, but with time I realized I didn't need to have a partner—I could be happy in myself. I had my music and took great joy in my family and friends.

For the March break in 1996, Julie and I visited Brian and Lesley in Tobago. We stayed in a sprawling house on a golf course with them, their two children, and another family. Tobago was beautiful, and they were so hospitable. We had a great time.

In August 1997, I visited Julie in British Columbia. She had finished university and was waitressing at a restaurant in a resort town near the Rockies. After a few days there, we drove west to Vancouver and then got the ferry to Vancouver Island. Audrey and Joe had retired there years before, but Audrey had since died. We arranged to meet Joe and had a good visit. I regret that I didn't go to visit them when Audrey was still alive. Both were so good to me when I was young.

Before and after my separation, I often visited my brother Bob and his family in Napanee. They were also very good to me. Once when I was visiting and Mother was present, I suddenly heard, "Dad didn't have one iota of love!" At first, I didn't know where it had come from. Then I realized with horror that *I* was the one who had said it. The words had gushed out of me like a volcano erupting.

On September 12, 1997, Steve married a girl named Lynn. The wedding was held at The Doctor's House in Kleinberg. We had the rehearsal dinner at the McMichael Gallery.

After Steve, Lynn, and Julie had graduated from university, the three of them rented a place near my High Park house. I remember jogging down to the lake and then stopping off at their place on the jog back. They were preparing for a party and had invited some friends of theirs I hadn't seen for a long time. I hung around for a while, waiting to be invited, until it occurred to me that they didn't want me there! I realized things had changed. They were now independent, and I had to be too.

CHAPTER 16

Sudden Retirement

When I was having trouble paying my mortgage due to lost income because of vacant apartments and the strike, I lowered Joc's support payments. She was furious. I got a letter from her demanding that I pay all *her* taxes on the support payments I'd given her, and warning me that if I didn't, she'd report me to Revenue Canada for giving her support payments without having a legal separation agreement. My lawyer said, "She can't do that! We're in negotiations!" However, she followed through on her threat, and I had to pay back the tax reductions I'd claimed for the previous two years.

When my friend Marilyn heard about my situation, she generously offered to pay for me to have a one-hour consultation with her lawyer, who was a tough negotiator. I hired him, and he sent me to a bankruptcy lawyer, who advised me to retire so that Joc's support payments would be based on a much lower income. I sold my house. I'll never forget Steve's response when I told him that I was sorry he wouldn't be inheriting the house: "That's OK. I'd rather have you than the house."

I found an apartment downtown to rent, retired, and declared bankruptcy. Joc and I went before a judge, who decreed that my support payments should stay the same and that she would get the marital home because it was roughly equal to the value of my pension. This didn't seem fair to me because I had to give Joc a big chunk of my pension in support payments!

I retired in October 1998, after 31.2 years of teaching. Barb, who had been appointed head of ESL, arranged a retirement party for me in the music room at Hart House, where I used to play the Steinway piano when I was in university. I was surprised how many people attended. There was a full dinner followed by several speeches, including one by Steve, who "roasted" me, which everyone loved. Mr. Baine and my friend Josh also attended. Barb and I played a duet on the Steinway, and then I played a solo.

My principal, Verna, attended. At one point she took me aside, clasped my hands, and said, "Grant, please come back and complete the semester!" I didn't know that I could teach after retiring. I told her my mother was visiting for two weeks, but I would come back after that. I was so glad I'd be able to finish the semester with my classes.

Two weeks later I went to Central Tech and tried to enter the ESL office. The door was locked, and I no longer had the key. When I knocked, a stranger opened the door and reluctantly let me in. Later I jokingly told a friend that I should have said, "Do you know who I am?"

He said, "No, you should have said, Do you know who I *was*?"

The following school year after I had *really* retired, I was surprised to get a call from Verna. She asked me to give the address to the graduates at Central Tech's commencement in November 1999. I was reluctant, but I liked her so much, how could I refuse? I thought a lot about my life and what I'd learned that might help the graduates, and then I worked hard at preparing a speech and actually enjoyed delivering it.

A few years later I encountered Verna at a retirement party. I had heard she'd been promoted to superintendent. She told me that she still remembered my speech and said it was the best commencement address she'd ever heard.

CHAPTER 17

Professional Pianist

One of the first things I did after retirement was give a recital with Barb. It was part of a series to raise money for a church—the first recital I'd played that required paid tickets to attend. Just before that, Marilyn had met a man named Roy who had a Steinway piano, and we formed a piano club that met about four times a year at different members' places.

I also took a course called Landmark, which gets people to articulate and confront their problems. An example I'll never forget was a young man who complained that after a painful breakup with his boyfriend, all his father said was, "Good! Now you can find a nice girl." He hadn't spoken to his father since. When the course leader heard that the man had only one sibling, a brother who had died of AIDS, he exclaimed, "How could you be so cruel, cutting your father off after he'd already lost his other child?" The young man continued to try to justify ending the relationship, but the leader talked him into contacting his father. The next day the young man told us he'd called his father and they had reconciled.

For the last day of the course, we had to write a letter to

someone. Inspired by the young man's experience with his father, I wrote a letter to my father asking for forgiveness for my part in our terrible relationship. Even though I had a release of emotion that day, the next day I felt nothing. I'd wanted to have an experience of reconciliation like the young man had, but there was never any connection between Dad and me to be broken or reconciled. And it wasn't because he was dead. He'd always been dead to me. I have no idea who he was. Despite decades of physical proximity, he had managed to completely hide himself from me.

I did further courses at Landmark and became much more open about who I was and what my aspirations were. I told the class I was a pianist. As a result, a line producer in the course arranged to have Jane Seymour come to my apartment to learn to mime playing the piano for a movie about a pianist that was being filmed in Toronto. (She had been one of the first Bond girls and then starred in a popular TV series.) Having a famous actress come to consult me as an "expert" did wonders for my ego!

In my final Landmark course, we had to do a project. Mine was to take music to seniors. I performed at a few seniors' homes but settled on one called The Gibson. I gave monthly recitals there for many years. I got great satisfaction out of playing for the seniors. Some of them counted the days until my next concert. I played a lot of songs from the thirties and forties, music from their time, and they loved it.

Landmark made me more outgoing. When I was chatting with a man at a party in the summer and mentioned that I played piano, he said he knew someone who had a restaurant named Gatsby's, which had live music, and he'd mention me. Soon I got a call to play the Friday after Labour Day, the beginning of the first school year when I wouldn't be returning to the classroom. I raced around looking for appropriate music. I had some light classical pieces I could play and made arrangements of a few popular songs.

On the night I was to play, my friend Hannes came to the restaurant. After I finished playing, I was just going to go home, but Hannes pushed me to ask Camillo, the owner, if he wanted me to play again. With limited enthusiasm, Camillo said yes, and this was my entry into playing professionally! I bought hundreds of dollars of fake books (books with just the melody, chord symbols, and lyrics) and worked all my waking hours making arrangements of popular songs!

For popular music, I decided not to take the typical jazzy approach of most lounge pianists but instead use an almost classical approach. When I was young, I'd heard a recording of Don Shirley playing popular music in a classical style, sometimes even incorporating actual phrases from classical music. One song I remember was "Night and Day," arranged like the "Moonlight Sonata." I absolutely loved that recording! It inspired me, and I tried to emulate Shirley's approach.

After I'd played at Gatsby's for a couple of months, a man named Ivan from MCCT came to hear me. He worked in special events at the Bay and asked if I'd play there for two weeks in December. I played mostly Christmas music for ten days, six hours a day, and got paid $30 per hour cash. It was very low pay, but it was what I wanted to do, and I didn't have to declare this income and give part of it to Joc and my creditors.

The following spring, Ivan called me and asked if I'd play three days a week at "The Room," an area in the Bay where they sold fur coats and expensive women's clothes. It was located next to where all the perfumes and colognes were—not an ideal location because the young people who worked at the booths often played loud music. However, I tried to play my very best and got a lot of praise. My boss got me to wear a tuxedo, which seemed to impress people. One woman said she bought a fur coat because of my playing, and that pleased the managers.

Sometimes I covered for one of the pianists playing at The Arcadian Court, an elegant dining room on the eighth floor of the Bay, with beautiful chandeliers and an excellent grand piano. I loved it because people came there to dine and listen to a pianist, and there was no competing music or noise. However, the pay was still $30 per hour, as opposed to the $130 per hour I could have got teaching ESL at a community college, but I vowed that no amount of money would ever lure me away from music. I turned down a principal who called to offer me a teaching job for half a year that would have paid me $40,000.

I enrolled in a course in popular music composition at the Conservatory. A singer named Lorraine Lawson came to talk to the class one evening. After she spoke, I went up and asked her if I could give her my card. I didn't expect anything to come of it, but a few weeks later, a woman named Mrs. Flannery called. She said Lorraine had mentioned me, and she asked me if I'd play at a house party she was giving. It turned out that she ran a travel company. Not long after the party, she called and asked if I'd play piano on a train for a tour crossing China on The Silk Road. The tour, my airfare, and meals would be paid for, and I'd get a little spending money as well. Gatsby's was about to close, so the timing was perfect. Our flight was on September 16, 2001, five days after 9/11. Because we were going to fly to the border with Afghanistan, which the United States planned to invade, we thought the trip might be cancelled. However, it went ahead, and only our guide and a couple of guests cancelled.

We flew to Vancouver and then Shanghai, where we stayed for a couple of days. Then we took a Chinese flight to Urumqi in the extreme west of China, right on the border of Afghanistan. We boarded a bus that took us through the foothills of the Heavenly Mountains to Heavenly Lake, which was stunningly beautiful. Returning to Urumqi, we boarded a train called the China Orient Express and began our trip eastward. I played in the bar car on an upright piano, just like the one in Mrs. Flannery's home.

Our first stop was Kashgar. The people who live in that part of China are Islamic Uighurs. In the morning we went to the Idkan Mosque. In the afternoon we went to the Sunday Bazaar where there were hundreds of animals for sale. A bull escaped and came charging toward us, but our guide gave it a swift kick and saved us!

Kashgar is very primitive, and we had two culture shocks there. First, some of us went over to see a camel near our hotel, and its keeper castrated it right before our eyes! Second, for our roasted lamb banquet at the hotel, the chef came out of the kitchen wheeling a lamb, lying on its back, legs up in the air, its head still on, and a large butcher knife in its throat! After a lot of whispering, Mrs. Flannery spoke to the head waiter and he wheeled it back into the kitchen, re-emerging later with it minus the knife in its throat.

Our guide, Yusef, explained that China had a one-child policy for Han Chinese, but a two-child policy for Uighurs. He told us education starts in Uighur, but later, Chinese as a second language is learned. (These privileges he was so pleased with seem ironic now considering China's current oppression of its Uighur minority.)

We headed east on the train, stopping for a few days to stay at the Silk Road Dunhuang Hotel and visit the sand dunes and Mogao Grottoes, one of the most important groups of Buddhist caves in the world. Then back on the train to Xian, an ancient walled city, where we went to see the Terracotta Warriors. Our last stop was Beijing, where some of us climbed the Great Wall of China.

When I returned to Canada, Gatsby's had closed. I looked for other places to play, but 2001 was a bad year for luxuries such as dining with a pianist playing in the background. Several places were recommended to me, but I would arrive only to find that they had discontinued having piano music. I supply taught for a while but always chose playing at the Arcadian Court if one of the pianists couldn't be there.

Julie, who had returned to Toronto, wanted to be a police officer, but I tried to point her to other, less dangerous careers. She took an ESL teacher's course, and I tried unsuccessfully to get her to go into teaching. Then I got her an interview for a job as parole officer. However, before the interview took place, I was walking west along College Street one morning when I saw an attractive, professional-looking young woman coming toward me and realized it was Julie! She had just successfully interviewed for a job with Toronto Police Service.

She went to train at the Ontario Police College, and in the target practice part of the course, her marksmanship was so good her instructor called his colleagues over to witness it. Jeff drove me to Aylmer for her graduation in May 2002. I'd never seen Julie so happy before. We drove her back to Toronto and on the way, we stopped at a nice restaurant and had a celebratory dinner.

Mother's health started to seriously decline. Her legs swelled up and discharged and they had to be bandaged twice a day.

Bob and I took her to the hospital once to have her legs looked at by the doctor. As the nurse removed the bandages carefully because they were tearing the damaged skin underneath, she said, "Oh, Mrs. Reynolds, I'm so sorry," her eyes filling with tears. However, Mother, very brave, steeled herself and had no reaction except for quick intakes of breath.

When she got even worse, Mother wanted to come to Toronto and stay at Sharon House, advertised as "a haven for healing for those relying solely on Christian Science treatment and prayer." There were problems getting her admitted, but Steve stepped in and convinced Sharon House to take her. He lived in Ottawa at the time and drove to Napanee to pick up Mother and then on to Toronto to pick me up and go to Sharon House. After a couple of weeks there, Mother wanted to go back home, so my brother Bob came to get her. She continued to decline, so Bob hired a personal caregiver who lived with Mother all week, and every weekend I went on the train to Napanee to care for her. Once I heard her say on a call with my brother, "He waits on me hand and foot." I wondered why she couldn't show me some gratitude or appear happy to see me.

Around this time, I ran into the partner of the man who owned the Steinway. He told me Roy was close to death. Roy died soon after, and his partner asked Barb and me to play at his funeral. Roy's two sisters from California were in Toronto to attend their brother's funeral and seemed to appreciate our musical contribution.

One Friday evening I arrived in Napanee and found out that Mother had died that afternoon. The caregiver said she had suddenly just started crying and then died. My brothers and I arranged a service. I played music on my keyboard, and my brothers and I did readings.

Looking back, I realize that Mother did absolutely everything she could for me. I remember her filling the fridge with low-calorie Jell-o and puddings when I was young, allowing me to buy the expensive edition of Beethoven's Sonatas when the cheaper one would have been just fine when I was in high school, and staying up late to type my essays when I was in university—anything she could do for me short of being demonstrative in expressing her love.

I've seen so many families divided over inheritances, but Mother had always been scrupulous in treating us equally. Each of her three sons got exactly a third of her estate.

Mother died shortly after Roy, whose partner called to ask if I wanted Roy's huge library of sheet music. When I asked what he was going to do with the Steinway, he said that Remenyi's Music had made a low offer. I took my piano technician over to look at the Steinway. When I asked if I should buy it, he said, "A Steinway is always a good thing." Steinways are expensive, but I got a reduced price, perhaps because Roy's partner and his sisters appreciated my playing at the funeral. I was able to buy the wonderful instrument with the money I had inherited from Mother.

Previously, I had seen an ad on TV for Plan Canada, which supports children in Third World countries, and I vowed that if I inherited any money from Mother, I would sponsor a child. When the money came through, I called Plan Canada and sponsored my first child. Over the last twenty years, it's given me joy and satisfaction to sponsor several others.

The year 2004 was very eventful. Steve and Lynn had a son, Mitch—my first grandchild! I went to Ottawa a few times to visit, usually on the train. I remember one time Steve picked me up at the train station with little Mitch sitting in the back in his car seat.

After a few minutes of driving, Mitch looked out the window and started singing. We often went to a park near Steve's house, where I would throw Mitch's soccer ball and we'd race after it to see who could get it first, but when we had almost reached it, I would trip and fall and Mitch would win, laughing his head off.

Steve was so generous. I remember once he drove me to the train station, and as he was driving away, he yelled, "Check your right coat pocket." I did, and there was the amount of money I'd spent for my train trip. Laughing, he sped off, knowing I couldn't catch him and protest.

Also in 2004, one of the pianists at The Arcadian Court asked if I wanted her Mondays. I was thrilled! Mrs. Flannery wanted me to go on another trip to a different part of China, but I turned her down just to be able to play at The Arcadian Court one day a week!

One December evening as I was heading out the door to play a gig, the phone rang. It was Bob's son calling to tell me that my brother had been in an accident. I played the gig and then raced home to call and found out that Bob, who worked for Bell, had been in his cherry picker installing telephone lines near the highway when a car slid off the icy road and hit his truck, throwing him up in the air. With no helmet on, he had landed on the ground and hit his head.

The next morning, I called Julie and Steve to tell them about the accident. Julie said she'd be right over to drive me to the hospital in Kingston. We pulled up to the hospital at exactly the same time as Steve arrived from Ottawa. Bob was in a coma for a while, and after he came out of it, he went through all kinds of therapies. Eventually there was a settlement, and he was awarded enough money to take care of him for the rest of his life. His wife had a home built with a lift and special accommodations for him, but he couldn't manage there, so he went to live in a home with other brain-injured men. My heart broke for Lynda and their four children.

The man whose car had slid into Bob's truck was Indigenous. He lived on the reservation near where Bob was doing the work. The Indigenous police arrived first and tested the man for alcohol and drugs but lost the test results. This looked suspicious, as did the fact that, as our lawyer pointed out, one of the investigating police officers who lost the tests had the same last name as the man. The accident had taken place around noon, and it was thought he had been sent home from work because he was drunk. He was found guilty of careless driving causing bodily harm, but because he had young children, he was allowed to serve his sentence at home.

The judge ordered a "healing circle." It was held on the reservation and included Bob (in a wheelchair), his wife and daughter, his brothers, his best friend, the man who had caused the accident, his mother, and three Indigenous social workers. One of the social workers led the healing circle. She got each of us to talk about our reaction when we'd heard the news about Bob's accident, and what Bob meant to each of us. I choked up as I told the group that Bob was the glue that held our extended family together. The social worker then questioned the man who'd crashed into Bob's truck about what he'd done and how he felt about it. After the man spoke briefly and with almost no emotion, she said, "Look at Bob. You *hurt* him. How do you feel about that?" After the meeting was over, we all shook hands with the man. I was so impressed with the lead social worker and how effective the healing circle was. It wasn't about religious denial. It was about facing the reality of Bob's tragic brain injury and expressing our deepest emotions and grief about it.

Around this time, I was at a party talking to someone about music when I noticed a man listening with interest. Soon he came over and joined the conversation. His name was D'Arcy, and we became good friends. He lived in a beautiful house in St. Catharines and played piano. Every summer I would visit him during the Niagara Music Festival and we'd go to hear recitals. Later he joined our piano club and would come all the way to Toronto for our get-togethers.

I invited Jeff to attend our piano club. He didn't play but enjoyed hearing the music. In 2004, he expressed his gratitude by generously paying to rent a hall for us to have a recital. We scouted out recital halls and found the Heliconian Club. (I had played there as a teenager in John Leberg's recitals.) For ten years we gave an annual recital there, raising money for the Regent Park School of Music.

I'd kept on playing Mondays at The Arcadian Court, and eventually the pianist who'd given me her Mondays quit altogether, so I got to play several days a week. We were allowed to put on recorded music and take short breaks, but I never did.

Playing requests was difficult, but I always took my little fakebook with 1,200 songs in it, and people usually seemed happy with my rendition of their favourite music. I remembered the music people had requested and often played their favourite piece when I saw them again. At home I practised a lot, continued making arrangements, and combined songs into medleys, which people loved.

Some customers gave me extravagant praise, saying I was the best pianist they'd ever heard, and I got many tips in my tip jar, sometimes even twenty-dollar bills. One woman asked me if I'd made any CDs. I hadn't, but her question made me think maybe I should. She kept asking me when my CD would be ready, but when I finally had an expected date, she said, "I could be dead by then!"

I got in touch with the man who had recorded our Heliconian recitals and had him bring his recording equipment to a church in West Toronto that had a glorious nine-foot Steinway and was often used to record in.

In 2006 I recorded my first CD, *Music of the Night*, and in 2009, I recorded my second, *Enchanted Evening*. I always kept a few CDs on the piano and was pleased how many people bought them.

Customers were given surveys of what they liked and didn't like at the Arcadian Court. I got so many good comments on my playing that I was given the Director's Award.

I also got asked to do a lot of special events, like weddings, for which I got paid well. I remember that two weeks after playing at an opulent wedding at Casa Loma, for which I'd already been well-paid, the bride sent me extra money with a note saying how pleased she was by my music.

At the Arcadian Court one day, a man who looked familiar came up to the piano and said, "We think you're wonderful!" I realized it was Ken Thomson, the richest man in Canada, who owned the paintings in the Thompson Galleries upstairs. Roy Thomson Hall was named for his father. His wife, Marilyn, had studied piano, and later on she came up and we had a conversation about music. When Ken Thomson died in 2006, I was invited to the service for him at Roy Thomson Hall, which included the beautiful slow movement of Mozart's clarinet concerto with soloist and full orchestra, and songs by Rita MacNeil.

Playing at the Arcadian Court was great! I loved making music, and many people loved hearing it. This did wonders for my self-esteem. With my new identity as a professional pianist, I moved out of my past life into a happier present.

In 2010, Compass Foods took over the Arcadian Court from the Bay. We could sign on with them or quit. I signed on and continued playing. Then one day in 2011, I got a call to come in for a "meeting." When I arrived, there was no one else there. It was exactly like the movie *Up in the Air*. A bouncer-type asked me if I was Grant Reynolds and said, "Come with me." He took me to a room where a man sitting at a table proceeded to tell me I was being terminated. Then he left and a woman came in and said comforting things about employee retraining, etc., after which the bouncer reappeared, told me to get all my belongings, and escorted me out the back way.

The Arcadian Court dining room closed, and it became exclusively a venue for special events.

CHAPTER 18

Andre

Jeff, who lived close by, invited me to many parties around this time, and I always hoped a man named Andre would be there. He was tall and thin with dark hair and dark, intense eyes. He was friendly to me without being flirtatious. When Jeff threw a goodbye party for a friend who was leaving Canada, he hired a male stripper to perform for us, but I remember being more interested in looking at Andre fully clothed than the naked stripper.

Andre sometimes had us to his loft for dinner, and once I invited him to a concert at Roy Thomson Hall. He showed interest in the music, even though classical music was not his thing, and he seemed fascinated by the architecture of Roy Thomson Hall, which he'd never been in before. We'd gone out to dinner beforehand, and he'd mentioned that a big celebration was planned that summer for his parents' fiftieth wedding anniversary, but it might not happen because there was talk about them separating.

Andre already had a university degree. When he decided to quit his job to study civil engineering full-time at Ryerson, I was impressed with him for boldly following his passion.

Jeff had moved back into the triplex where his aging mother lived, and he invited me to dinner there on Friday, April 8, 2005. When I arrived, I was pleased to see Andre there. After dinner we played cards with Jeff's mother, and then Andre asked me if I'd like a ride to the subway. As we got close to where he'd let me off, I realized this was the perfect opportunity. I steeled myself and nervously blurted out, "Andre, can I ask you something? I know you're busy with university, but would you consider dating? You don't have to answer now. Thanks for the ride." Then I jumped out of the car.

I was so surprised when he called the next morning! He said, "In light of what you said last night, would you like to come to dinner tonight?" I couldn't because I'd been invited to a birthday party that night, but he said, "How about Sunday?"

Andre had made a delicious dinner, which we had with a bottle of red wine. Afterwards I was very nervous because we were already part of a group of friends. What if the sex didn't work out? How embarrassing it would be to re-encounter him. But sex was great, and we got together frequently.

A couple of weeks later, Andre had Mike, a friend from Sudbury, to dinner and invited Jeff and me. After dinner he drove Mike to the airport. Since it was early, Jeff and I decided to wait for Andre to return. At a certain point, Jeff asked, "What's with you and Andre?" I think he was hurt that I hadn't told him about our new relationship, but Andre and I are both private people, and I had wanted to wait longer before telling anyone.

After a month or so, I asked Andre if I could refer to him as my partner. I was delighted when he said yes. In September he asked me if I'd go to his sister's in Elliot Lake for Thanksgiving with his family, saying, "I've never brought anyone home before." That really pleased me! I felt so honoured.

Andre has a big, warm French-Canadian family. At Thanksgiving dinner, we were about fourteen in number. Unlike Andre, who is rather quiet and admits, like me, to being introverted, others in his family are outgoing. They made me feel very welcome. After dinner, Andre's father started singing a song he'd taught his children when they were young (with actions like tapping your fork on a glass), and everyone joined in. There was a piano at the end of the large dining room, and I announced that I wanted to play "La Vie en Rose," dedicated to Andre. We stayed at his sister's place. That night when we got into bed, Andre gave me a big kiss and said, "Thank you!"

The next morning as I started down the stairs, I could hear everyone in the living room speaking animatedly in French. When I was halfway down and they could only see my legs, without missing a beat they all switched to English in order to make me feel included. Andre's parents headed back home to Sudbury, but his sister had Andre and me to their cottage on Dunlop Lake, not far from the town of Elliot Lake.

When I got back to Toronto, I told Julie about Dunlop Lake because she had been interested in buying a cottage, but anything near Toronto was prohibitively expensive. Julie looked it up on the internet and soon bought a lot on Dunlop Lake.

A few months later, Andre's sister invited us to stay at her cottage for a week. Andre and I went with Steve (who had moved back to Toronto), three-year-old Mitch, Julie, and Jeff. We had a great time! After our long drive back to Toronto, we finally arrived at Steve's house, where Jeff had left his car. When Jeff said goodbye and started heading to his car, Mitch raced up to him and jumped into his arms, much to his mother's surprise and delight.

When I got to know him, Andre told me about riding with his arms around his father's waist on a motorcycle trip around Lake Superior when he was young. I thought that kind of connection with your father would be wonderful. He also told me that when he came out to his parents, *they* were the ones who went for counselling, not him, which really impressed and moved me.

I had always pretended that my relationship with my parents was good. I wanted them to be like Andre's parents, but after hearing these things, I could no longer continue pretending. It wasn't just Andre's parents. The more parents I got to know and see in action, the more I realized how cold my parents were, and how sad I felt about my childhood.

In 2007, Andre graduated with honours from Ryerson University. At his convocation, I sat with his father. When Andre went up to get his degree, his father exclaimed, "Andre is brilliant!" Although I was happy Andre had such a supportive father, I felt a little sad because I couldn't help comparing him to my father.

Andre's parents did finally separate, and one day in 2008, he told me his sister had indicated that his mother wasn't doing well, and he would be moving back to Sudbury to help her. He said that he'd understand if I didn't want to continue the relationship. It crossed my mind that maybe *he* would like to end the relationship, but he'd always said what he meant, so I assured him I wanted to continue our relationship. He moved to Sudbury in September, and several times a year he would drive to Toronto to visit me, or I would take the bus to Sudbury to see him.

On September 4, 2010, Andre called to tell me that a very close friend of his had died. I'd spent time with her twice when she visited Andre in Toronto, and I liked her. At a later date,

Andre and I had visited her in Sudbury, where I met her husband, but he was getting ready to go hunting and didn't spend much time with us. Andre told me that she had given him some things she didn't want her husband to have if they separated.

She did tell her husband she was leaving him…and he stabbed her to death. The funeral was a week later. Two seats at the front of the packed church were reserved for us. Later, Andre had to testify at the husband's trial. He told me how awful he looked, and a year or two later he died in jail, presumably of suicide.

When Andre had gone to Sudbury to help his mother, he told his father, "If you needed me, I'd do the same for you." His father had moved to Sarnia, and when Andre heard something was wrong with him, he immediately went to look after him. It turned out his father had brain cancer. When it got very bad, Andre brought him back to Sudbury, where he died in November 2010. At the funeral home, one of Andre's lovely nieces pinned a button on me that indicated I was part of the family. Many people attended the funeral. Always generous, Andre's father had arranged and paid for dinner and an open bar for everyone after the funeral.

CHAPTER 19

Religion

When I started playing at Gatsby's, I had to give up the MCCT choir because I could no longer attend Thursday evening choir practices. Soon I also stopped going to Sunday services because I saw more and more examples of how fundamentalist mainstream Christianity is. One Sunday, another minister substituted for Brent Hawkes. After telling us the Noah's Ark story, she actually stated that God was so sad about drowning people, he decided never to flood the world again. Despite Christian Science's absurd exaggeration of the connection between how we think and our ability to heal ourselves, at least it's reasonable in maintaining that biblical stories like Noah's Ark are just fiction.

Years later I played in two recitals at an Anglican church around Eastertime, and I had to sit through the services that came before. Each time the minister called us "sinners," which I found very offensive, especially as there were children present.

In January 2011, I saw an article about a Canadian organization called Centre For Inquiry (CFI), which was about to place an ad on TTC buses, that read: *Extraordinary Claims Require*

Extraordinary Evidence

Allah. Bigfoot. Homeopathy. Zeus. Christ. Psychics

This got me thinking about the importance of evidence and how there is no evidence for the existence of gods or an afterlife, and yet religions continue to devalue this life by considering it a mere prelude to an imagined afterlife.

When I was twenty-four, I had felt alone in my new-found atheism, unable to develop my thinking much beyond simply not believing in God, but at last I'd found a group that would support my thinking and allow me to develop my ideas.

I started subscribing to two American magazines: *Skeptical Inquirer* and *Free Inquiry*. I also joined the Freedom from Religion Foundation (FFRF), an American atheist organization that fights for separation of Church and State.

I did a lot of reading and thinking about religion, and came to the conclusion that it is a desperate attempt to avoid facing the difficult reality that we live in a universe that is totally indifferent to us, and that because religions contradict reason, science, and each other, they are often criticized and then proceed to do whatever is needed to silence critics, including execution, as widely practised in historical Christianity and modern-day Islam.

I also came to realize that we just *think* we live in a secular society, but so many good ideas are still suppressed by religion that, if it weren't for atheist organizations and publications, we would never even know that these ideas existed.

Through CFI, I went to hear a great presentation by James Randi, the man who had exposed both faith-healer Peter Popoff (on the *Johnny Carson Show*) and illusionist Uri Geller.

I also attended a CFI-sponsored debate about religion with two professors I'd never heard of. One was arguing for religion; the other, against. By the end of the debate, the one arguing for religion was red-faced with anger, furiously marching around the stage as his opponent made convincing arguments against religion.

Soon after the debate, I was surprised to see the professor who'd argued for religion on TVO—surprised because in the debate he had shown how limited he was. I found out his name was Jordan Peterson. Later I was shocked to learn that he wrote a best-selling book.

CHAPTER 20

Performance Master Class

When The Arcadian Court closed in 2011, it wasn't that bad for me because I'd played professionally for twelve wonderful years.

In September 2012, I enrolled in Boyanna Toyich's Performance Master Class at the Faculty of Music, U of T. I'd heard of it when I was at CTS and had gone to see Boyanna give a presentation on it after I retired, but playing at The Arcadian Court had made it impossible for me to take the Master Class. There were about a dozen students, and four of us would typically play every class. Boyanna was very knowledgeable about piano literature and technique but also very affectionate and funny. Once when it was my turn to play, she asked, "OK, *cupcake*, what are you going to play for us today?" You couldn't take offence because you knew she loved you. Every spring we had a recital at Walter Hall, playing on a glorious nine-foot concert Steinway. Boyanna was always backstage with us, encouraging each performer.

I took the course for eight years and learned so much.

Through connections in this course, I had a chance to take some lessons from Leo Erice, a superb pianist and wonderful teacher, until he moved to Ottawa.

In 2017, I made my third CD of popular music, *From Gershwin to Andrew Lloyd Webber*, consisting of twelve medleys, each with three songs. I wanted to polish up my arrangements of the best of the popular music I had played at The Arcadian Court and get them recorded before I forgot them. I also wanted to incorporate what I'd learned in Boyanna's class. I practised very hard and was pleased with the result. My new CD was much better than my previous two CDs of popular music.

After completing the CD of popular music, I started working toward making a CD of classical music, practising harder than ever before.

In 2019, Boyanna got so ill she could no longer teach the Master Class. A pianist named Asher Armstrong took over for her and led us through our May 2019 recital. I went to hear his Brahms recital, which was excellent, and started taking private lessons with him. Both Asher and his wife taught at the Faculty of Music, so I thought I could count on him being my teacher for a long time.

We were all shocked when in June 2019, we heard that Boyanna had suddenly died. She had taught at the Conservatory and Faculty of Music for over forty years. Her funeral was packed with people who came to honor her.

In September, the Master Class started again under Asher's leadership, and I continued taking private lessons from him. His teaching helped me a lot, and his enthusiasm about my playing really inspired me.

CHAPTER 21

Travel

While working with the Toronto Police Service, Julie had bought a townhouse in Etobicoke. After buying the lot on Dunlop Lake, she switched to the Barrie Police Force, sold her townhouse, and bought a detached house in a beautiful area of Midhurst. She met another officer named Bob, who eventually moved in with her. Now they live in a gorgeous six-bedroom home across the street from the first one. And they also have a beautiful cottage on Dunlop Lake, that Bob built.

The year 2012 was great for travel. In January, Andre and I went to Costa Rica with Julie, Bob, and Bob's two teenage children. Julie had found a mansion to rent at the top of a small mountain near the town of Atenas. It was paradise! It had a beautiful pool, which magically wound around, parts of it hidden by bushes. Andre and I had our own separate suite. The climate was perfect. Being on a mountain, it never went above a dry thirty during the day, and it went down to a comfortable twenty at night. Every day oranges were picked and left for us so we could make fresh orange juice. And we could walk to a waterfall right on the property.

By this time, Steve was very successful financially. A pharmaceutical rep with a good salary, he also got many bonuses for his high volume of sales. Whereas other reps took doctors to sports events, Steve thought of taking them to the Toronto Symphony (after a dinner at a fine restaurant). I got to go along as a kind of music consultant.

In February, Steve took me to Cancun. The trip was for the top performing salespeople in his company and their partners, but Steve and Lynn had separated, and he happened to have no girlfriend at the time, so he took me. I'd never experienced such luxury before. Every single thing was paid for by Steve's company. There were five or six world-class restaurants in the compound. Each of us had a special activity we could choose. I chose a helicopter trip, flying over the coastline with beautiful views of the beaches below.

In June, Andre's mother took her five children and their partners on a cruise to Les Isles Madeleine. Our ship left Montreal and headed up the St. Lawrence to the Gulf of St. Lawrence near Prince Edward Island. Les Madeleines are seven islands. We explored the islands during the day and slept on the boat at night. One evening we went to an excellent restaurant to celebrate Andre's mother's eightieth birthday.

Julie had been pregnant when we went to Costa Rica. On April 13, 2012, she gave birth to a daughter, Lexie. Two years later on April 15, 2014, her son, Liam, was born. She said she wanted a sibling for Lexie because she and her brother were so close.

On the afternoon of May 19, 2014, I had just changed into my gym clothes at the Central Y when I lost consciousness and fell to the floor. There was no pain, no warning. When I came to, I was lying in a bed in the dark. A woman's voice said, "You had a cardiac arrest and are now in the ICU at Toronto General Hospital." She proceeded to ask me my name, what year it was, and what I remembered from just before the cardiac arrest to ascertain if there was any cognitive loss, but luckily there was none.

The next day a policeman arrived and gave me the names and telephone numbers of the two men who had saved my life. Later, someone asked about Steve, the contact person I had written down. They couldn't reach him. *How unusual*, I thought. *Steve is always available.* (It turned out he was climbing in the Grand Canyon.) He appeared the next day and called everyone to tell them what had happened to me. Soon Andre arrived from Sudbury. I gave him the keys to my apartment, and every day he rented a bicycle and rode over to visit me. I had two stents put in and was to have a defibrillator implanted, but I got an infection and had to wait until it was gone to have the operation. I was in the hospital for four weeks instead of one. I had several roommates. The last one was named Paul. After we got out, we became friends.

Andre had gone back to Sudbury after a week but came back when I was to check out. After a month of breathing hospital air, it was thrilling to breathe fresh air as he wheeled me out to the parking lot.

Eventually I contacted the two men who had saved me. The first was a nursing student, who saw me fall and applied CPR immediately. The other was the Y lifeguard, who rushed down to continue CPR and shock my heart with a defibrillator.

Only a small percentage of people who have a cardiac arrest survive. If I'd been alone in my apartment, which is true for me most of the time, I'd have died. Also, only a small percentage of those people who do survive retain full cognitive functioning so I was doubly lucky. A few weeks after I got out of the hospital, I thanked the two men who'd saved my life and gave each a gift. Later they were presented with awards by both Toronto Paramedic Services and Toronto Police Services.

Ten-year-old Mitch came to the Toronto Paramedic Services Awards. Afterwards, he wrote about it for his Catholic school: *"When my grandfather dropped into a cardiac arrest and a life guard sprang to his feet and imediately attended c.p.r. without damaging any parts of his body, my grandfather's heart started beating again! That man is a light of the world!"*

In November 2014, Steve and Julie had a seventieth birthday party for me at Steve's house. They gave me two return tickets to San Francisco, the place both Andre and I had most wanted to visit.

In September 2015, Andre and I flew to San Francisco. We stayed there exploring the city for about a week, taking a trip to Alcatraz and visiting Castro Street, the Golden Gate Bridge, and Fisherman's Wharf. Then we rented a car and drove to the Monterey Bay Aquarium, the Hearst Castle at San Simeon, Yosemite Park, Sacramento (the capital), and Lake Tahoe. I was most interested in San Simeon, but Andre loved the Redwood forests most. It was such a wonderful trip. We saw so many beautiful spots, and now when I see California in films, I can relate to it.

That fall, Steve's cardiologist discovered that he had an aortic aneurysm. He had to have open-heart surgery, which terrified me. What if he didn't survive? I couldn't bear that thought. I went with him to see Dr. David, the world-class surgeon who would be operating on him. He told Steve, "Normally it's a fairly safe operation, but you have the complicating factor of cardiomyopathy."

The surgery took place on October 21, 2015. Julie, Steve's

friend, Marcos, and I sat nervously in the waiting room, hoping Steve would be OK. After a few hours, Dr. David, came over to us and said that the operation had gone well. Steve stayed in the hospital for a few days. I took Mitch to see him once. When Steve got out of the hospital, I stayed at his house for about three weeks to take care of him.

Soon after Steve got home, an elaborate gift basket of wonderful treats arrived for him. It was from Yvonne. Shortly after I had sold my house and moved to my apartment, I had run into her. It had been many years since I'd seen her, but I reconnected with her and her husband, Aubrey. They hired me to play for their fiftieth wedding anniversary and came to hear me play at Gatsby's, The Arcadian Court, and the Heliconian concerts. Other times we would go out to dinner, but first they would come to my apartment and I would play for them. If it was a popular song, Aubrey could name it and even recite the lyrics.

In March 2018, I went to London with Steve and Mitch. We spent one day with British friends of Steve's, riding on the huge Ferris wheel that provides such a great view of the city and going through the very interesting Science Museum. Steve, Mitch, and I are big fans of Winston Churchill and were fascinated by the Churchill Museum. We had boat trips on the Thames and bus trips through the city. One evening after dark we had a guided tour of exactly where Jack the Ripper had committed his various murders. The guide made it really scary. We also enjoyed the Sherlock Holmes Museum, which made you almost believe he was real.

For meals we experimented with numerous eating places. We walked everywhere, and sometimes crossing a road was really dangerous because we weren't familiar with British traffic rules. Steve was like a father trying to keep his two kids safe.

Mitch almost got hit once. On one occasion, I thought I heard Steve shout "Cross," but in the middle of the street seeing a bus barreling toward me, I realized he'd said "Bus!" Luckily, I was able to safely run to the other side of the road. We laughed so much about it afterwards. I will never forget that trip. We had so much fun.

After Steve had separated from Lynn, he'd bought a small bungalow in a great area of Etobicoke and eventually had it knocked down. He and his new partner, Kim built a large, six-bedroom house on the property for themselves, Mitch, and Kim's two daughters.

Mitch had started school in the French Immersion program, but he found it very difficult. After a few years, he switched to Extended French (half French, half English). Unfortunately, Extended French was only available in the Catholic board, so Mitch had to switch from the public board. He now had to go to chapel and take religion every year. Steve saw this as an opportunity to educate Mitch about the huge gap between what the Catholic Church says and what it does, and the pedophilia, homophobia, and corruption so widespread in the religion. Steve, a qualified high school teacher, helped Mitch with his schoolwork, and his marks improved every year. Steve got me to go over to their place and help Mitch with French and English once a week.

When Mitch was very young, his parents had brought him to The Arcadian Court to hear me play. I still remember him staring intently at me as I played the piano. As I had with Steve and Julie, I took him to the TSO Young People's Concert Series for five or six years, and he seemed fairly interested. Near the end of the first concert, he whispered to me that he had to go to the bathroom. I knew the concert was almost over, but I couldn't take a chance, so we headed to the basement washroom. While we were there, the huge sound of the final applause came over the intercom, causing Mitch to exclaim, *"It's not fair!"*

When he was six, I bought Mitch a keyboard. He started piano lessons but didn't continue very long. Once, when we were at Julie's, I was asked to play. After I'd finished, eight-year-old Mitch surprised everyone by asserting that *he* wanted to play! He sat down at the piano and moved the fingers of both hands in pianistic ways, making pleasant, atonal music! Later on, he started taking guitar lessons, and I was able to help him with aspects like rhythm. As time went on, music became a real bond between us.

Near the end of Grade 8, Mitch was in a talent show at his school, and I was invited. I thought he was going to play a guitar solo, but when he went to perform, he took a big breath and started *singing,* accompanying himself on the guitar. I didn't even know Mitch sang, and I couldn't believe how good he was. He had a pleasant voice, and he sang right on key. His song was so good that the recording of it was played at the end of the year as the Grade 8 graduates marched out of the school.

Mitch was full of surprises. I didn't know he had any interest in drama, but he auditioned successfully to get into the drama program in a special arts school. In the summer before Grade 9, he went to a camp for an orientation to his new school. Then just after he started Grade 9, he was chosen to speak about the camp at a fall assembly to introduce the school to prospective students and their parents.

Mitch got a part in the school drama production (unusual for a Grade 9 student). In the summer he took a course in musical theatre at Stratford. He met an actor he'd never heard of named Danny DeVito, who was very critical of him, but Mitch wasn't fazed. He wrote back stories for some of the characters in the play, causing DeVito to say, "You know, kid, at first I thought you were crap, but you're not so bad." The following school year, Mitch got a lead part, Prince Charming, in his school musical, *Into the Woods*.

In October 2019, Julie organized a trip to Disney World for Lexie, Liam, her friend Lindsay, Andre, and me. We were to be there on October 31, and Lexie and Liam cried because they would miss Halloween trick or treating at home. However, we had many different rooms to hide in, so we bought candies, and the kids dressed up in their Halloween costumes and had a great time knocking on the various doors in our rented townhouse and getting treats from each of us.

The rides were terrifying. We got on a rollercoaster that began slowly then started climbing higher and higher, but soon the tracks just ended, and if we'd kept going, the train would have flown off the end and crashed to the ground. However, suddenly the train started racing backwards at a breakneck speed. I thought I was going to have a heart attack! Later I was "captain" on a simulated space flight with missiles hitting our spaceship and shaking our seats so much that we could hardly remain in them. I glanced over at the other captain, a young man, who looked just as frightened as I was.

I was to turn seventy-five in November (2019) and didn't want to celebrate it, but Andre was insistent, so I organized a dinner at the Grand Hotel. Julie brought table decorations, Bob showed a hilarious video, Steve was MC, and Mitch gave a wonderful tribute to me.

I spent Christmas with Julie, Bob, Lexie, and Liam and had a great time. Andre was to come to Toronto for New Year's as usual. However, he got sick and couldn't come, so I went to Jeff's annual party by myself. It was fun but not the same without him.

The year 2020 did not start well and got so much worse. On January 18, I woke up to water streaming into my kitchen sink from between the cupboards above. I notified the super and called the emergency number. A plumber came in the afternoon and stopped the leaks. However, the next morning I woke to find water running down the kitchen wall. Above the cupboards was massive crumbling drywall, and I thought the cupboards were about to fall off the wall. I called emergency again and took everything out of the cupboards. Again a plumber came and stopped the leaking. (On February 3, I had my regular defibrillator check, which showed that on January 20, the day after the weekend leaks, my heart had fluttered for seventeen hours!)

Around that time I got sick. On January 24, I went to my doctor, who said I had pneumonia and put me on antibiotics. Soon I could smell mould and had more and more trouble breathing, especially in the kitchen. On February 5, I wrote the office: *"It is urgent that the mould be removed now!"* Eventually the mouldy drywall was removed and a new kitchen was built.

Shortly after this, Bob called to tell me that Julie had a lump in her breast. I was devastated because years ago I had two women teachers in my department, both with young children, who were diagnosed with cancer. After radiation and chemotherapy, they became cancer free, only to have it return in a couple of years and kill them. I feared the worst and was unable to bear the thought of losing Julie. Soon after, unaware that Bob had already told me, Julie visited to tell me the news herself. To my great relief, the lump had been discovered early, and Julie was arranging to have a lumpectomy.

Remembering Joc

Joc had suffered from COPD for many years. At one point, she had come to West Park, a rehab centre in Toronto, swam every day, lost weight, and seemed to improve dramatically. However, when she returned to Elmvale, she started putting on weight again. Her breathing got so bad she always had to have oxygen. She would drive to and from Julie and Bob's in Midhurst (about twenty-five miles away) for special celebrations, and we'd all worry about her having an accident. Everyone was surprised how friendly Joc and I were on these occasions. We would spend a lot of time talking to each other, although when Andre came on the scene, she switched to talking to him instead of me.

Eating seemed to be Joc's only comfort, and I remember noticing her once at Julie's dining table after we'd all finished our dinners, lovingly cradling the plate with the remaining cake on it, her arm wrapped around it protectively.

She went back to West Park, hoping to improve as she had the first time, but her health was so bad she was placed in the hospital wing. On March 25, 2017, at a family celebration at West Park, she couldn't breathe and had to be rushed to the hospital. The next day she wanted to go back to West Park, but they wouldn't take her because they couldn't deal with such a serious illness.

Four days after being admitted to the hospital, on March 29, she was close to death and asked to see Mitch. Steve got him out of school and brought him to the hospital then called me to see if I could take Mitch home afterwards and stay with him. I went to the hospital and arrived at Joc's room to see her periodically taking morphine for the pain and sometimes nodding off briefly. When Mitch leaned in to kiss her goodbye, she told him what a good boy he was and that she loved him, but when *I* leaned in to say goodbye, she said, "Well, it's been a slice. Where's Andre? I really like Andre." I went back to Steve's with Mitch, and that evening Steve called to say that Joc had died.

Steve and Julie arranged a celebration of Joc's life a week later. They asked me to speak, and I said: "In talking about Joc, I'll try to abide by the rule, 'If you can't say something nice, don't say nothin' at all.' But I have to admit I haven't always followed that rule. Once, when I was complaining about Joc, my wonderful friend Barb said, 'She can't be that bad. Look at Steve and Julie!' That gave me pause. I had to admit Joc was totally devoted to them when they were young. She spent all her time looking for books to read to them, enjoyable books with life lessons. And I've never heard a better reader. She thought of activities for them that they would enjoy and learn from. And most important of all, they always knew she loved them."

Steve and Julie also spoke. I hadn't discussed what I intended to say with them, and I'm not sure they conferred with each other, but we all said essentially the same thing: Joc had been a wonderful mother when they were young.

Joc's older brother in Calgary sent Steve and Julie an email after Joc's death:

"I wish to commend you for your untiring efforts to help Jocelyn through the most difficult time in her life. Reflecting on the last ten years or so, Jocelyn proved to be a tough fighter, trying desperately to retain some control of her life, and this spirit sometimes was an obstacle to those determined to help her. The fact that you persisted in the face of adversity and made great progress in making her last years rewarding and as comfortable as possible is more than noteworthy. From conversations I had with Jocelyn in the recent past, it was clear that she was devoted to her children and grandchildren, and very proud of all of you. She always spoke fondly of the opportunities you provided for her to be with 'the kids.' We are very grateful for your efforts.

"Please pass this message on to your father, whom I have not seen in many years, and who is to be commended for his continuing patience and support for Jocelyn through difficult circumstances."

When Steve and Julie were older, I was surprised at how *badly* Joc treated them. I thought they were both wonderful. I couldn't imagine having better children. One year, I sent Joc a Mother's Day card, thanking her for giving me Steve and Julie. Joc wrote back to me: "Thank you again for the lovely Mother's Day message—I think what makes it so special is that it is a real gift from the heart and one that could not be given to anyone else—better than flowers or even Andre's chocolates. Something I can pull out and savour whenever I wish, for the rest of my life."

Joc had two sides to her. I used to think of the nursery rhyme: "When she was good, she was very, very good, but when she was bad, she was horrid." Julie had told me that in one of her courses, she had come across a mental illness that perfectly described her mother: borderline personality disorder, which causes a person to have stormy relationships with others, often radically switching from closeness and love to hostility and hate.

I now had an explanation for many of Joc's formerly inexplicable thoughts and behaviours. She was clearly intelligent, and it always baffled me that she couldn't see the obvious. She hungered for human contact but couldn't help driving everyone away from her.

She and her mother would have frequent fights and stop talking to each other for extended periods of time. One fall early on in our marriage, I remember thinking her relationship with her family was finally over, but on Christmas Eve, her parents paid a surprise visit, loaded with Xmas gifts for us, and everything was lovey-dovey again. This happened often.

Once I taught piano to a twelve-year-old girl who was fond of me (as students often are of their teachers). Joc just couldn't stop talking about what a flirt this innocent little girl was. When we were visiting my parents, after listening to Joc rail about the girl, Dad stated the obvious: "You're jealous of her." I was so embarrassed that my wife couldn't even hide her furious jealousy of a twelve-year-old girl!

At CTS once I was having trouble with a difficult girl who was constantly disrupting my class. I told Joc about it, and she was very explicit about the punitive measures I *must* take with her. Every night as soon as I got home, she would grill me about what I'd done and then give me instructions about the next step to take in subduing this girl. I used nasty disciplinary tactics that were completely not my style. The whole class turned against me, and a family member came to the VP with complaints about how I had treated this girl (the only time in my entire teaching career that I got a complaint about my teaching). Needless to say, I never told Joc about a teaching problem again.

The film *Play Misty for Me* is the only time I've ever seen a character like Jocelyn portrayed. In the film a woman stalks the Clint Eastwood character, and without warning she even arrives at his place with groceries, planning to set up house. Later on, she sees him with another woman at a business lunch and has a furious temper tantrum. The film took me back to my early days with, Joc who, when we got two separate apartments, never stayed in hers for one minute. She just moved into mine, took charge of everything, and was constantly exploding with jealousy (curiously only about other women, never men).

After the Celebration of Life, I began to realize that after forty-eight years, my worrying about what Joc was going to do next was finally over. Also, I no longer had to pay support payments, and her will had one third of her estate go to each of us: Steve, Julie, and me. (I suspect Julie talked Joc into including me in the will because Joc had a house and a car, and I had neither.)

Joc and I had a terrible marriage! I felt she hated me, but once at a family gathering after we had separated, she looked at me with the same warm smile she had when we first met and said, "We should have just been friends."

CHAPTER 23

COVID

On the afternoon of March 12, 2020, Steve and I went to the hospital to get Julie after her lumpectomy. We were in her room when the announcement came that Premier Ford was extending the March Break because of COVID. Julie checked out of the hospital, Steve drove us to a restaurant, and the three of us had a wonderful time having a meal together. Steve said he didn't want me to go through the stress of driving to Midhurst and back to take Julie home, so he let me off at a subway stop.

Only when I got home and watched the news did I realize that this was a serious pandemic! My Master Class was the next day, so I emailed Asher and the class that I wouldn't be attending because, being elderly and having heart disease, I was vulnerable to COVID.

So many things ended because of COVID: teaching piano lessons; taking piano lessons from Asher; playing in my two piano clubs; my weekly Master Classes; my weekly trip to help Mitch with his schoolwork; my weekly psychiatrist appointments; my monthly massages; going out to movies, dinners, and recitals; and visiting Andre.

I felt bad for Mitch. The musical he had a lead part in was cancelled, his second course at Stratford was cancelled, and there would be no 2020/21 drama or musical at his school.

Steve and I both started FaceTiming Julie to talk and read Lexie and Liam stories. I could see how difficult having the kids home was for Julie after just having had her operation.

I continued working intensely on my coming classical CD. For the first time in my entire life, I had as much time to practise as I wanted! I kept thinking of what Barb had said years before when she was volunteering at the Pan Am Games: practising the piano is like training for an Olympic athletic event.

Steve was very good to me. Every other day he would come over (often with Mitch and his dog, Oreo) and we'd drive to Chorley Park and walk through The Brickworks, enjoying the wildlife, other dogs, and the beautiful scenery. Steve and I share a deep interest in film and politics, and we had great conversations on these walks. Mitch, with a passionate interest in film and unusual sophistication for a boy of his age, would join in whenever films came up for discussion.

In April, Steve, seeing on the news that my area had a lot of COVID cases, insisted that I move to his house. On Saturday, April 4, I gathered the things I would need and moved. Ever since my pneumonia and the mould in my apartment, I'd had more and more trouble breathing.

For some reason, perhaps allergies, I got even worse at Steve's house. On my fifth night at Steve's, after struggling to breathe all night, I woke Steve up at 5:00 a.m. and asked him to call an ambulance. On the way to the hospital, the ambulance attendant asked me about my symptoms. When I told him, he said, "It feels like you're drowning, right?"

I said, "Yes, exactly!" I was taken to Etobicoke General

Hospital and had a catheter put in me. After a few hours, passing two litres of water, and getting a prescription for water pills, I left the hospital with Steve, who drove me to his house to get what I'd brought and take it all back to my apartment. He was disappointed, but what a good sport!

The next week was Easter, and I was happy to be by myself. Seven days a week I practised two to four hours in the morning and early afternoon, as much as I can do in one day.

However, I realized I also had the time and energy to do a second project . I had recently read *Educated* by Tara Westover and was inspired by how much she had achieved despite her very difficult childhood. Before that I had read Daniel Goleman's *Emotional Intelligence* and was struck by how much parents like mine who lack emotional intelligence can damage a child. I also wanted to tell the story of how music had given me so much joy and helped me get through difficult times.

I decided to write a memoir. After an early dinner, I would sit down at my computer and start writing. Sometimes it was depressing to focus on my life, but usually writing my memoir seemed to validate me and, to some extent, help me overcome my feelings of worthlessness and shame, perhaps because through writing about them I was distancing my life experiences from me as though they belonged to someone else. .

Julie gave a lot of thought as to how she would deal with her cancer. She wanted to be as sure as possible of getting rid of it, and on June 12 she had a mastectomy. She was in the hospital for three days, after which Bob and the kids came to Toronto to get her.

On December 6, one of my piano clubs had a virtual recital. Steve managed the technical side, but when I came to play, I had no energy and had to substitute a slow piece for the two fast pieces I had intended to play. I was getting weaker and weaker, had trouble breathing, and could only walk at a snail's pace. My cardiologist told me that the two ventricles of my heart were beating out of synch, and that hopefully my current defibrillator could be replaced by a "cardiac resynchronization therapy defibrillator" with three leads to the heart (instead of two) that would resynchronize them.

On January 5, 2021, I had a venogram to see if my veins were in good enough shape to have the special defibrillator put in. The surgeon, Dr. Noad, called me the next day to say that my veins were fine and to answer questions about the surgery. I was very impressed with her.

January 28 was my day to have the surgery. At 8:00 a.m. I changed into a hospital gown and was directed to a bed. Dr. Noad came over and introduced herself. A few minutes later, the nurse who was to put the IV in asked me if I had good veins in my hands. I said, "Yes, I'm a pianist." On hearing this, Dr. Noad came over again and told me that she also played the piano. I asked if she liked popular music, and when she said she did, I asked a nurse to pass me my backpack and presented her with my CD, *From Gershwin to Andrew Lloyd Webber*. She seemed pleased and said, "Gershwin! I'm learning 'Rhapsody in Blue'!"

The surgery was very painful. My head was covered so I couldn't see, but someone, presumably Dr. Noad, pressed down on my upper chest with incredible force. I now believe she was pushing the new defibrillator down into a new pocket under a lot of fat, muscle, scar tissue, and veins. The previous one had been so close to the surface that there was concern it might come out. This one certainly wouldn't.

The next day, Dr. Noad came by to see how I was doing. She thanked me for the CD, and said she had played it when she got home and was inspired to practise. She looked at the wound and said everything looked fine. Steve came to drive me home later that day.

I was in a lot of pain for a few days, but soon I was breathing comfortably again. After a week, Steve and Mitch came for a walk, and I could climb hills and breathe with no struggle and no pain.

On February 15, my psychiatrist, Rick Lamon, called to say that he had advanced Parkinson's disease and wouldn't be able to see patients anymore because there were signs of dementia. I was so sad because he's such a kind man and deserves better. All I could do was write him a letter of thanks and tell him how much he'd helped me.

I saw a sign in my pharmacy about vaccinations against COVID and signed up. Julie and Steve were both against my getting the vaccine because it was AstraZeneca. Before I could get the shot, Julie called me to say that she'd gotten an appointment for me to get the Pfizer vaccine, and on March 25, I went to the Metro Convention Centre and got my first shot.

In late May, four months after my surgery, my left arm and hand started to swell up, and in a couple of days they were twice as big as my right arm and hand! I worried that I might never be able to play the piano again. I got Steve to take me to Emergency at Toronto General. All manner of tests were done, and I was taken up to the cardiovascular ICU. Many doctors (Steve counted twenty-three) were involved in my unusual case. Eventually it was discovered that one of the leads from my new defibrillator had punctured a vein and an artery.

My first surgery (on June 1) was four hours long. Afterwards I was hungry, not having eaten anything for twenty-four hours. Steve was visiting as I ate my dinner. Perhaps in my hunger and talking to Steve, I didn't chew my food properly. In the middle of the night, I aspirated and had a breathing tube put down my throat. When I came to, Julie was holding my hand. I thought it was the next day and was horrified to find out that I had been unconscious with the ventilator in me for three days! Julie and I had a five-hour visit, which felt so good. I was moved to the fourth floor, and she carried my belongings to the new room before saying goodbye.

That night I lay in my hospital bed thinking about how much love and concern for me Julie and Steve had shown. I also thought of all my wonderful friends, like Barb, and vowed that if I survived this ordeal, I would try to show them more love.

My second surgery was June 5, but the problem was still not solved.

My third surgery was to be on June 9, but on June 8, just after I had eaten lunch, an orderly walked into my room and said, "We're here to take you to surgery." I thought they must have made a mistake in the date because you're not supposed to eat anything for many hours before surgery, but after two unsuccessful operations, I was so desperate to have the problem fixed that I said nothing.

After the surgery, the doctors told me they had finally been successful. I was wheeled back to my room and felt great for a while, but soon I started burping and felt like throwing up but couldn't. My digestive system just stopped. I had to have a tube shoved down through one of my nostrils (and then taped to my nose) to take out the contents of my stomach. It was one of the ghastliest experiences of my whole life. After about twenty-four hours, the tube was removed. Steve, who knows a lot about medical issues, told me my gastric problems came from having surgery right after a meal.

On June 9, an "abdominal wall hematoma" (a large blood blister) appeared on my left side, and I wasn't able to leave the hospital until June 17. Every day the nurse gave me a needle in my stomach to prevent blood clots, and I was to give myself the needle every day for three months after I got home.

When I was finally allowed to leave the hospital, Steve drove me home and stayed the night to make sure I was OK, and Julie came from Midhurst to stay the second night with me, bringing all manner of foods.

I was totally surprised and delighted when a gift basket arrived. It was from Yvonne, of course!

One of the things required by the hospital was for me to see my GP after a week at home. At my appointment, my doctor said she had watched all the steps in my hospital stay with horror, and she told me I was incredibly lucky to be alive. This was the second time I had escaped death, and it made me realize that every day was precious and I had to make some important changes. I tried to call friends and family more often, pick up when they called, and enjoy talking to them rather than resenting the time it took away from my piano practising and writing.

CHAPTER 24

Anxiety Disorder

A few years ago, I needed a letter from my psychiatrist to get out of jury duty. He wrote: "He has experienced anxiety symptoms his entire life and he has the DSM 5 diagnosis of Generalized Anxiety Disorder."

This was the first time I had seen my psychological problem named. I did some research and discovered that some of the causes of anxiety are: disapproval of a significant adult, an equally shy and inhibited parent, and being continually belittled or devalued in the family.

All of the above describe my childhood.

Much of the time it's very uncomfortable to be me.

At my nephew's wedding a few years ago, I was fine for the service because I didn't have to make conversation. However, at the reception I had to interact with many people, and free-flowing conversation always causes anxiety in me. For some reason, this particular reception was very uncomfortable for me. I was aware of how I couldn't relax, and that I must look as nervous as I felt. When someone took a photograph of me and said, "You look like a serial killer," it made me even more distraught, and I was tense for the entire evening.

When I was living in the basement apartment, I remember telling a friend that I was interested in buying an income home. He said, "I'll introduce you to a real estate agent I know. You'll get along really well. He's *stiff,* just like you." I was taken aback because, although I was aware of being uptight and socially awkward, I didn't know it was *that* obvious. I tended to under-play, and sometimes even deny, my anxiety.

I never felt any shame about seeing a psychiatrist. People close to me knew about it, and several friends had even asked me about Dr. Lamon and then gone to see him. However, I remember when another teacher saw me standing on the oppo-site subway platform from the one I usually took to get home and asked me where I was going. When I said I was going to see my psychiatrist, she said with obvious disappointment in me, "I'm surprised that *you* would be going to a psychiatrist!"

In early July 2021, after I got out of the hospital, I was to play at a Zoom recital of Master Class students. Because of the pan-demic, we hadn't met for well over a year. Barb was organizing it, and the day before the recital when I called to tell her what I'd be playing, she said my three pieces might be too long because we all needed time to reconnect socially. Hearing about the *social* focus of the recital caused me not to sleep that night. The next day I called Barb and told her about my anxiety disorder (the first time I'd ever told anyone) and said I wouldn't be joining the Zoom meeting.

The next Master Class Zoom recital was in September, and I decided I had to play. I was afraid that if I didn't, I might never rejoin the Master Class students. When we started the recital, I felt exactly as I had at the wedding reception. Not only did I have trouble thinking of what to say, but by the time I unmuted the iPad, the conversation had moved on to a different topic. It was so nerve-wracking because the only person I could see was the one playing or talking, and I didn't know if others could see me. I had the strange feeling that they were in a movie I couldn't be in, or swimming freely in a fishbowl I couldn't get into.

At the October Zoom Master Class recital, again I *forced* myself to play. My fingers felt as if they were covered with maple syrup. I washed my hands twice, but I couldn't get the stickiness off. Tremendously nervous, I began playing. My hands were shaking, and I even had to stop and start again at one point (very unusual for me). I felt totally demoralized afterwards and had trouble sleeping that night.

In the morning I felt depressed until I remembered one of the women in the group speaking about my performance. She had tried to say nice things, but her tone of voice and facial expression indicated how appalled she was by my playing. I chuckled a lot thinking about this, and it got me over my depression.

A sense of humour is often my salvation!

CHAPTER 25

Good Parenting

*"As a parent, my mother cared deeply for her children ...
One time, after I had children of my own and was unsure of
whether I was doing right by them, she told me that it doesn't really
matter whether you are permissive or strict, fun-loving or serious, as
long as they know you love them." (Hannes Kivilaht)*

It has always given me great joy to watch Julie and Steve bring up their children. When Lexie and Liam were toddlers, it was wonderful to see Julie's loving attention to them, and Bob coming home from work, changing clothes, and rolling around on the floor playing with them. I would think to myself, *This is what parenting should be—demonstrative! My parents got it so wrong!*

When they were a little older and I called or FaceTimed them, if I asked one of them "How are you?" at first there would be no response. Then I'd hear a very soft whispering from Julie and get a "Good. How are you?" response from Lexie or Liam. With time they became very communicative, expressive, and affectionate. Now they say "I love you" often and hug me warmly when I see them.

Steve's caring for Mitch has also been wonderful to watch. He's always thinking of what to teach Mitch about life. Steve wrote this letter to Robert Munsch, the author of *Love You Forever*:

"While I was listening to *Love You Forever* with my six-year-old son, Mitch, tears rolled out of my eyes and over my ears (I was lying on my back in his bed with him beside me). At one point I looked up and saw Mitch—his eyes as big as saucers—staring at me. After the book was finished, he cocked his head and asked, 'Hey, Dad, were you sweating?' I said, 'No, I was crying because I love that book so much.' I'll never forget his response: *'Dad, when I grow up, I'm going to cry just like you.'*"

After Joc moved to Elmvale, Steve used to take Mitch there to help maintain her property. Once he was trimming hedges, and Mitch was assisting. Joc always liked to supervise, and Mitch sometimes blocked her view. She kept yelling, "Get out of the way!" Finally, Steve stopped the trimming and said, "OK, Mitch, Grandma's getting grumpy. It's time to go." Without any angry words, they got in the car and drove back to Toronto. Steve told me he wanted Mitch to learn to help others but also to have enough self-respect to refuse to take abuse.

Every experience was turned into a lesson for Mitch. Once Steve and Mitch ran out of gas on the way to see Julie and Bob in Midhurst. Steve said calmly, "Well, what should we do, Mitch? Should we call Bob and have him bring gas?" He was showing Mitch that problems have solutions.

I wish that my parents had been like Steve and Julie. I wish they had shared themselves with me and taught me lessons about life. I wish they had told me what was right about me, not just what was wrong. I wish they had held my hand, patted me on my shoulder, or hugged me. And most of all, I wish they had shown me that they loved me.

CHAPTER 26

Looking Back On My Life

Recently I've felt a need to look back on my life and attempt to understand it. Sometimes it's been very difficult to do, but it's also been liberating. Telling my life story has released me from some of the shame I felt and given me a new perspective. Some of the things I've come to realize include:

I've had a mental illness ever since I was a child. There may be a connection between how I was treated when I was young and this mental illness, but whatever the cause—my parents, my homosexuality, genetics, or all three of them—I've always had an anxiety disorder that separates me from others. While it couldn't be cured, it could, to some extent, be mitigated. I'm lucky in that I found a very supportive psychiatrist. Over the twenty-five years of weekly sessions, I got so much help from him. But I also did *my* work: figuring out what I needed to talk about and face up to in my life and doing it.

Christian Science was very harmful to me. Instead of facing my problems, I escaped into a solitary make-believe world when I could have been learning how to relate to others. And I still have to fight a tendency to deny problems rather than admit them and deal with them.

My homosexuality has been very destructive to me. I grew up in a world where it was absolutely unacceptable, and I will always carry deep shame about it and feel alienated and different from others.

My relationship with Joc was a *choice*, not an accident, as I had always thought. When I first met her, I was emotionally dead and was drawn to her because she was expressive and vibrant, and I needed her to open me up to life.

I thought high school teaching had been the wrong occupation for me because I'm an introvert, but I now realize that it was good for me because it forced me to come out of my shell and interact with others.

I tried to substitute *status* for the lack of love in my life. When I became a high school teacher, I wanted to be admired for it. And when I started teaching teachers and directing university courses, I worked frantically to succeed, always hungering for recognition. I could never feel valued for who I was, just for my achievements.

Music saved my life! As a child I felt unloved and worthless. My self-image was of a boy who failed in all the areas that mattered. My first step out of that sense of failure was the adulation I received for arranging and playing a duo-piano version of "Exodus" for my high school music night. The rest of my life consisted of more successes in music, right up to becoming a professional pianist. Music brought me so much joy and self-esteem. Although not a substitute for love, it was crucial in helping me survive because it allowed me to express emotions and feel that I had some worth.

These days I feel very lucky. At last I have time to thoroughly explore the world of music, and through music I can escape from my problems, but it's so much more than just an escape. Often I experience ecstasy and am carried away to another world. Playing the piano is perfect for me in that it's a very solitary pursuit, and to be comfortable I need to spend a lot of time alone.

I'm also incredibly fortunate to have two wonderful children, Steve and Julie. At the beginning of my life, I didn't feel loved by my parents, who strove not to be demonstrative, but near the end of my life, I have two children who constantly demonstrate their love for me. Also, I received nothing but disapproval from my parents, but my children almost always show approval—not necessarily of all my actions but of who I basically am. My present life is filled with love—not that this can change my past, but to love and be loved at last is a wonderful kind of redemption.